52 WAYS TO
OUTSMART THE IRS:

WEEKLY TAX TIPS TO SAVE YOU MONEY

ROBERT F HOCKENSMITH, CPA, EA, MBA

Published by:
Robert F Hockensmith, CPA, EA, MBA
3404 West Cheryl Drive, Suite A-170
Phoenix, Az 85051

https://azmoneyguy.com
https://52pickup.com
https://52waystooutsmarttheirs.com

ISBN: 9798601386128
ASIN: 8601386128

First Edition January 2020
52 Ways to Outsmart The IRS

"This publication is designed to provide accurate and
authoritative information regarding the subject matter covered.
It is sold with the understanding that the publisher is not
engaged in providing legal, accounting, or other professional advice
or services. If legal advice or other expert advice is required, the
services of a competent professional person should be sought."
From a *Declaration of Principles* jointly adopted by a
Committee of American Bar Association and a Committee of
Publishers and Associations.

Contents

INTRODUCTION

This is my second year at a writing for the public. My first book, *52 Pick-Up, Weekly Tax Tips to Save You Money*, was met with good results, so I have taken to heart some professional suggestions and am releasing this new title. *52 Ways to Outsmart the IRS: Weekly Tax Tips to Save You Money,* is full of updated content, for 2020.

I spent 6 years in the military before going to college. I didn't finish high school before enlisting in the military during Vietnam. In fact, during basic training a few of us grunts were selected to combine basic training during the day and study for the High School Equivalency, General Education Development (GED) certificate, at night. What a feeling of accomplishment I had when, upon basic training graduation I was also awarded my GED the same day. Though I felt like I climbed a mountain that day, I still felt that I wasn't really a high school graduate. So, I found out what was needed to get a high school diploma and I took classes while in the military, at night, to be able to obtain one.

I was awarded a high school diploma in 6 months after basic training. That's when the bug hit me. The education bug. Imagine how dumb I felt when I didn't know something that my friends' thought was common knowledge. I was embarrassed to say I didn't understand, so I would just listen in, write down the subject and head over the library as soon as possible, to learn what my friends were talking about. It got to the point that I found myself enjoying reading and learning new concepts and ideas. **To put this in perspective, there were no laptops, tablets or desktop computers to reference. There was no internet in 1972! You had to read real books to learn something!**

I started taking night classes at a local community college and correspondence courses on all kinds of general subjects. Soon I investigated what it took to attend college full time, and I started planning on when I would leave the military and become a full-time college student. I started my college journey toward getting a degree in Computer Science because I thought, in 1978, it was the future. While moving toward my degree I had to take an accounting class.

To my surprise, I understood and enjoyed the subject. I know, who enjoys accounting? Me. I liked the logic, structure and order that accounting offers, obviously from my military background. I found out that I could get a dual degree in computers and accounting so that's what I did. I worked as an accounting intern during college on a work study program. The local CPA firm hired me because I had worked with radios, telephones and early mainframe computers while in the military, and they were adding automation to the firm. It was a win for both the CPA firm and me. When I graduated from college, I was the first person in my family to attend and graduate with a degree.

Since then, I haven't stopped learning. I went on to complete a master's in business administration (MBA), specializing in Economics. Finally, I attended Law School, just because I liked the challenge and thought it would help me in my practice. In Law School, to explain or defend my clients' tax returns, I learned how to prepare an argument or defense, and put the points in logical order with IRS references and specific cases. Today, I log over 100 contact hours annually, learning new tax laws and ideas, to stay on top of my chosen profession.

I started preparing tax returns by hand, before tax software even existed. That was a great way to learn both the theory and the practice of taxes and accounting. Three (3) years into practicing tax return services, I passed the Enrolled Agent (EA) exam, and the next year I passed the Certified Public Accountant (CPA) exam. Both of those professional exams were three days long!

Since then I have prepared thousands of tax returns, have represented hundreds of audited tax clients before the Internal Revenue Service (IRS), and have educated thousands of clients, students, and the public. I use my experience and education to look for ways that my clients can pay the LEAST amount of tax; legally! There are so **many** ways to accomplish this! I am constantly learning more and showing people how to save money. Whether it's saving money from taxes, economics, or finance. I have been practicing tax preparation, representation, resolution and advisory services and have been educating the public since 1984.

Most taxpayers do not understand taxes, which is why I wrote this book. After appearing on TV, radio and in print, for so many years and having taught accounting, economics, tax law, and finance classes, I have put together a collection of what I believe you can find useful as weekly tax tips. These tax tips are written in a format that everyone can understand, no matter what your tax knowledge level, from basic to expert. Each week's tip is written in a story line fashion and covers tax, economic and finance topics.

Some of these tips has been around for a long time but updated for the Tax Cut and Jobs Act (TCJA), which took effect January 1, 2018. Some tips are brand new, since the passing of the TCJA, such as the Setting Every Community Up for Retirement Enhancement Act (SECURE) of 2019 and the Taxpayer Certainty and Disaster Relief Act of 2019.

Whether old tips or new tips, you can benefit from reading and learning ways to cut your taxes and keep more of your hard-earned money for yourself.

As with all tax law, it changes constantly. This writing reflects the most up to date interpretations and explanations according to my understanding and interpretations of the rules and regulations of the Internal Revenue Service, for the tax year 2019. This means that you are reading this in 2020 or later.

Each week's tips can be used independent of the other weeks, so you don't need to read them sequentially. Many of these tips are related, but it's not necessary to read them together, in order to understand and implement the ideas, tips, and suggestions that are provided. Some of the tips can be used as stated in the book, while others might need further detailed explanations, catered to the reader's specific situation or circumstances.

These weekly tips are general in nature and explanation and should not be used in complicated tax, economic or financial situations, without professional help. Each week's tip should be checked for updates, before following them blindly. You should consider speaking with a licensed tax professional in order to explain specific or complicated circumstances. Look for a Certified Public Accountant (CPA), Enrolled Agent (EA) or attorney in your area.

Only CPA's, EA's or attorneys can represent taxpayers before the Internal Revenue Service (IRS).

I have borrowed, copied and paraphrased information from the IRS, SEC, Department of Labor, and many other government agencies and or documents, in addition to my own understanding of economics, finance and tax law.

It is my goal to show you that learning about taxes can be fun, entertaining and educational all at the same time. Learning can be eye opening and stimulating. I plan on updating this book annually as laws change. So be sure to look for my next updated edition. I hope you enjoy this book as much as I enjoyed writing it.

WEEK #1 – New Year's Financial Resolutions

It's a New Year, and for Dave and Julia, a married couple, the New Year also signifies a fresh start to financial responsibilities. Responsibilities that simply translate to financial commitments like an upgraded house to accommodate children, meet their demands of fancy toys and Disneyland vacations, start saving for their education and more importantly: Financial Freedom!

Now is the time to look at their finances, spending habits, debts, credit cards, insurance coverages, future, and activities that put them in the status and position they are in today. While Dave and Julia are not so unhappy with their financial situation, they strive to improve, because financial freedom is still on their wish-list.

Whether you are poor, average, (like Dave and Julia) or rich, everyone needs to look at their financial picture at least on an annual, quarterly, monthly or preferably every payday basis. **My best advice is to review your finances every payday**. Dave and Julia always do just that because it helps them renew or reinforce what they were doing and allows them an opportunity to correct bad habits that may hold them back from achieving financial freedom. The constant review of their budget, every payday, helps them know where their money is going, ahead of time. It's like looking out the windshield of a car, rather than looking at the rear-view mirror. Knowing where your money is going ahead of time, helps keep you on track, so your journey to financial freedom is a guided path, rather than a blind walk through life.

As with any successful accomplishment, you must start with a guide, plan, blueprint, charter, or budget! Use whatever word that helps you understand the need for financial planning consistency. Consistency throughout the 365 days in a year is key to financial freedom. Dave and Julia know that if something can help them start or continue their path to financial freedom, it is consistency in financial planning. Such a plan keeps you focused and on track towards the destination or in this case the 'journey' you travel. The same steps that help you lose weight, complete a college degree, or break bad habits are useful to begin improving your financial goals.

I have listed the top 6 steps to help you financially in the New Year. Following these will take you closer to financial freedom. They are:

Pay off Holiday debts

Should be done within 90 days of New Year. Plan a budget on how much you will spend and let each partner keep check on the other. Each person who writes down a budget has a better chance of sticking to it, rather than just talking about it, guessing or "trying it out". There is no try, there is only do or do not; remember that saying?

1. **Track your spending and create a budget**

   Keep every receipt for the first three months, for absolutely everything you spend. Budgets are made each payday; BEFORE you are paid. That way you know where every dollar will go, ahead of time.

2. **Start savings plan**

   New Year Holiday budget or keep your change in clear piggy bank. Remember the journey of 1000 miles starts with the first step. Always start a savings plan with an emergency fund, before you do anything else. This should be 3-6 month's living expenses and this fund is only used in an emergency (medical, fired from or quit work, car breaks down. **Only real emergencies**). You may need to work another job to save this.

3. **Pay down debt**

   Smallest debt first, then move up and pay the next smallest, and so on. While doing this, only make minimum payments on unpaid debt, until it is THE next debt on the list to pay off. While paying these small to large debts, don't worry about the interest rate on the debt, just the size of the debt. Often it is necessary to find more income so you can add extra payments to each debt being paid off. Most people have an income problem, not an expense problem. So, finding part time work helps pay down debt. Or selling items around the house provides extra income to pay down or off debt. Learning how to live on less is the key to paying off debt. **The fastest way to make money is to pay down, or off debt.**

4. **Review your credit report every 4 months**

   You are entitled to a free credit report from each agency annually -Transunion, Equifax, Experian. Requesting these helps prevent identity theft and improves your credit status if errors are found. **Remember, a free credit report does not mean a free credit score.**

5. **Check your insurance policies**

   Many people over-insure and under-insure property (car, house, contents, artwork, etc.). Talk to a planner who doesn't sell insurance to help you decide how much and what kind of insurance you might need. If you have someone who depends on your income, if you die, you need 7-10 times your annual income, for life insurance coverage. **And the only kind of life insurance to buy is level term life insurance.** No other kind of life insurance will work to help you find financial freedom. Most people over-insure their home. There is no need to insure land, just the replacement value of your home's building and contents.

Each step is independent of the other and can be started and continued its own. By completing each step regularly, you will see your debt go away, and your bank account increase. Remember that re-visiting, reviewing, and renewing your goals regularly will help keep you on track toward your financial success.

Robert F Hockensmith

WEEK #2 - Prepare for Upcoming Tax Season, request a Transcript or Copy of a Prior Year Tax Return

While the freshness of the New Year can still be felt in the air, let's start talking about preparing for the upcoming tax season. Dave and Julia know that preparedness always helps them in improving their performance for any tasks and makes their lives easier.

So, the first thing to do, is to take out last year's tax return and review it. Usually, taxpayers don't change much from year to year and the same kind of expenses are incurred every year. Next, they start organizing their expense receipts by placing different receipts in an envelope by category of expense, i.e. mortgage interest, real estate taxes, charitable contributions, W-2s, interest income, dividend income, and so on. Putting receipts in envelopes by category helps in visually categorizing your expenses, hence adding to your preparedness for the upcoming tax season.

You may need copies of your filed tax returns for many reasons. For example, they can help you prepare future tax returns. You'll need them if you must amend a prior year's tax return or apply for a loan to buy a home or to start a business. You may also need them if you apply for student aid. If you can't find your copies, you can request a

7

copy of previous tax return transcripts or actual copies of returns from the IRS. There is a fee the IRS charges for copies of actual tax returns (but not transcripts), check the IRS website **www.irs.gov** or contact your tax professional.

Here's how to get your federal tax return information from the IRS:

- A tax return transcript shows most line items from the tax return that you filed. It also includes items from any accompanying forms and schedules that you filed. It doesn't reflect any changes you or the IRS made, after you filed your original return.

- A tax account transcript includes your marital status, the type of return you filed, your adjusted gross income and taxable income. It does include any changes that you or the IRS made to your tax return, after you filed it.

- You can get them by phone, mail or fax within five to 10 days from the time IRS receives your request.

  - To request copies of your transcripts, go to **www.irs.gov** and use the **Get Transcript** tool.

- To order by phone, call **800-908-9946** and follow the prompts. You can also request your transcript using your smartphone with the **IRS2Go** mobile phone app.
- To request an individual tax return transcript by mail or fax, complete **Form 4506T-EZ**, Short Form Request for Individual Tax Return Transcript. Businesses and individuals who need a tax account transcript should use **Form 4506-T**, Request for Transcript of Tax Return.

- If you need a copy of your filed and processed tax return, it will cost a fee for each tax year. You should complete **Form 4506**, Request for Copy of Tax Return, to make the request. Mail it to the IRS address listed on the form for your area. Copies are generally available for the current year and past six years. You should allow 75 days for delivery.

- If you live in a federally declared disaster area, you can get a free copy of your tax return. Visit **www.IRS.gov** for more disaster relief information.

After you have copies of last year's return or transcript, contact your accountant or tax preparer as soon as possible and schedule an appointment. Most accountants pre-schedule their appointments and send letters out the first or second week of January. **If you wait until**

the last minute (late March or early April), you will end up paying more to have your tax return prepared. Tax preparers put a premium on the stress taxpayers place on them, by waiting until the last minute. So, Dave and Julia, did not make the mistake of waiting till the end, instead contacted their accountant at the earliest time in January.

Finally, if you have changed your name or marital status, let the Social Security Administration (SSA) and the IRS know about the change. If the name on the tax return does not agree with the Social Security number, both at the SSA and at the IRS, the refund for your personal tax return may be delayed, if not disallowed. This can cost a great deal of time, money and stress. The average taxpayer will lose about $1,000 in tax savings for each person that does not have a matching name and social security number. This also includes your children.

Here are some points to remember:

- Acquire and examine a copy of your last year's tax return or transcript to review expenses

- Categorize expenses with envelopes (i.e. income, mortgage expense, real estate taxes, auto tags, charitable contributions, medical expenses, etc.)

- Make sure you schedule your tax appointment early

- Verify with the IRS and SSA that names and social security numbers match (if name has changed)

WEEK #3 – E-Filing Advantages and Tax Return Headaches for Self-Filers

In an era of emails and e-tickets, e-file is the buzzword. Everything is joining the bandwagon of being electronically processed, to make it swifter, smoother and easier and this is true even for filing tax returns. All professional tax preparers are required to file the returns electronically (e-file), except for few options. You can even e-file your tax returns all year long. Don and Sherry are aware of this.

If you prepare your own individual tax return, you can choose to electronically (e-file) file it, or mail in a paper income tax return. And whether you prepare your own returns or engage a professional tax preparer, some tax returns still require a paper copy be mailed into the Internal Revenue Service (IRS). For instance, if you have an Adoption Tax Credit, or are sending in amended or past year tax returns older than 6 years from due date, your return must be mailed in. If you are divorced, and claim the Child Tax Credit and later find out that your ex-spouse claimed the child (even if they were not allowed to) and filed their return before you filed yours, you will need to send in a paper copy of your return with a copy of your Divorce Decree, and proof of Identification (i.e. Driver's license, Passport, State ID card, Military Id card). This is the only way to prove that you have the right to claim the child as a dependent and save on your income taxes. These are some of the reasons why you might still have

13

to file your tax return via US Postal Service. **And if you send anything to the IRS or any government agency, always send it certified mail, return receipt requested. This is a way to PROVE you sent the return to the IRS or state Department of Revenue.**

Electronically filing (E-File) is the preferred method of filing for the IRS. E-filing your tax return provides many benefits to you:

- You can save a copy of your tax return on a flash drive or hard drive, hence less paper for you to keep track of.

- Once you e-file your tax return, the IRS will respond to you via email within 48 hours, to let you know that your tax return was received and that it is accurate (math only) and complete (correct social security numbers). The IRS even tells you if something needs to be corrected and re-submitted, like with misspelled names or wrong names and social security numbers. When you try to submit your tax return with these mistakes, you will get a rejection notice, with an explanation of what is wrong. Then you can correct it and submit again.

- You will also be able to check the refund status of your e-filed tax return. Look under "Where's my refund?" at IRS.gov

- E-filing your tax return also means you will receive any refund quicker. Taxpayers that e-filed their tax returns, and used direct deposit, usually receive their refund within 10 days.

- You can also decide if you want to pay your tax with a credit card or an electronic debit from your checking account. **Be careful, both the IRS and credit card companies charge fees to pay income taxes.** Now you can see that sending your return using e-file is faster, easier to track, and allows for a quicker refund.

Note: if your IRS refund is $10,000 or more, expect your refund to be delayed up to 6 months while they check your refund for possible fraud.

Tax Return Trouble for Self-Filers

While many people self-file tax returns, it is usually better to use a professional tax preparer. This is true for many reasons. First, you are not a tax preparer. You do not scour over the tax code, read the rules and regulations, go to continuing education classes, pass hard, lengthy, expensive licensing exams and maintain professional licenses, like Certified Public Accountants, Enrolled Agents, and Attorneys do. These tax professionals save you much more than you know. The average self-filer brings home around $1850, while tax professionals help refund around $2650. Quite a bit more, huh? Once Don and Sherry found this out, they never tried to prepare their own taxes again. They even call their tax professional every time they think of spending money on big items, just to make sure they don't miss any tax saving opportunities!

There are many reasons why working with a tax professional can save you money. A tax professional will prevent you from making the mistakes that cost millions of taxpayers in overpaid taxes, every year. Such benefits of working with a tax professional aren't just about your refund. Think of all the time spent on reading the rules (especially this year), learning how to interpret and use them, knowing which documents are important for preparation of your return and which are not, knowing where you kept old copies when you apply for a loan, keeping up on any new tax developments regularly, and having someone you can bounce off ideas for financial decisions, BEFORE you make a mistake, and the list goes on. Tax Professionals are not just for wealthy taxpayers. Your tax professional should be able to save you more than they charge you!

What to Look for in a Tax Professional?

So, how do you find a tax professional? Look under Certified Public Accountants (CPA) and Enrolled Agents (EA). Both are tax experts. One is expert at both tax and accounting (Certified Public Accountant) and one is expert at only tax (Enrolled Agent). Always look for the license hanging in their offices. It takes years to become either one, so these professionals are rightfully proud to display those credentials. Both are much better at tax law than the national tax preparation service franchises.

Where do you look for a Certified Public Accountant or Enrolled Agent? You can google them in your area, but most will ask family and friends, who they use. Look for someone that cares about teaching you how to save money. A good tax professional should always go over your return and answer any questions before they submit your return to the IRS. Further, a good professional will keep you up to date on new tax developments. These professionals are experts in tax preparation, tax resolution, and tax planning. That means they can help you save on taxes every year. And if you are ever questioned about your tax returns, CPA's and EA's can legally represent you before the IRS! So, Don and Sherry never take a chance at self-filing. They always depend on a trusted licensed tax professional.

Tax season is in full swing, so finding a qualified, trustworthy tax expert will only get more difficult between now and April 15. CALL TODAY, don't delay!

WEEK #4 – Medical, Dental, and Health Deductions and Expenses

Did you know that you may be able to deduct expenses you pay for someone who is not claimed as a dependent? This week's tip is about medical expenses and deductions that some people are unaware of. **For instance, Dave provided over one-half of his mother's support for the past year, so he can include the medical expenses he paid for her.**

Below is an excerpt from the **IRS** about medical expenses:

"Medical care expenses include payments for the diagnosis, cure, mitigation, treatment, or prevention of disease, or payments for treatments affecting any structure or function of the body."

Medical care expenses include the insurance premiums you paid for policies that cover medical care or for a qualified long-term care insurance policy covering qualified long- term care services.

If you are self-employed and have a net profit for the year, you may be able to deduct (as an adjustment to income) the premiums you paid on a health insurance policy covering medical care, including a qualified long-term care insurance policy that covers medical care for yourself, your spouse and dependents.

To your advantage, you can also deduct some medical expenses paid for, even if you are not ill. In a ruling issued since 2007, the IRS concluded some unreimbursed medical expenses are deductible, even if you incur them when you are not sick. Examples include your annual physical check-ups, body scans, and pregnancy test kits.

Medicine you buy without a doctor's prescription is usually non-deductible; however, items such as crutches, braces, elastic hosiery, and blood sugar tests do qualify as expenses. Home health care items such as walkers, bed and chair lifts, and compression hoses also qualify as expenses.

If you, your spouse, or a dependent attend a conference relating to your chronic disease, the registration fee and travel expenses are deductible. Travel costs for medical care or treatments are also deductible, as are the travel costs for a caregiver who goes with you for care or treatment. Bob and Sharon live in Phoenix, Az and travel to San Diego, where they both grew up, to see their family dentist twice a year, and deduct the travel and treatment costs of the dental trip.

Let's look at some of the many medical care costs you may be able to deduct.

Deductible medical expenses may include, but are not limited to:

- Payments of fees to doctors, dentists, eye doctors, surgeons, chiropractors, psychiatrists, psychologists, and nontraditional medical practitioners.

- Payments for in-patient hospital care or nursing home services, including the cost of meals and lodging, charged by the hospital or nursing home.

- Payments for acupuncture treatments or inpatient treatment at a center for alcohol or drug addiction, for participation in a smoking-cessation program and for drugs to alleviate nicotine withdrawal that require a prescription.

- Payments to participate in a weight-loss program for a specific disease or diseases, including obesity, diagnosed by a physician but not ordinarily, payments for diet food items or the payment of health club dues. Health club dues may be deductible. See your tax professional for specifics.

- Payments for insulin and payments for drugs that require a prescription.

- Payments for admission and transportation to a medical conference relating to a chronic disease that you, your spouse, or your dependents have (if the costs are primarily for and essential to necessitated medical care). However, you may not deduct the costs for meals and lodging while attending the medical conference.

- Payments for false teeth, reading or prescription eyeglasses or contact lenses, hearing aids, crutches, wheelchairs, and for service animals for the blind or deaf (including all costs for feeding, housing, care and medical costs, of service animals).

- Payments for transportation primarily for and essential to medical care that qualify as medical expenses, such as, payments of the actual fare for a taxi, bus, train, or ambulance or for medical transportation by personal car, the amount of your actual out-of-pocket expenses such as for gas and oil, or the amount of the standard mileage rate for medical expenses, plus the cost of tolls and parking fees.

- **If you are a business owner, partner, or shareholder of an S-Corporation you can deduct your health insurance premiums (including Medicare insurance) on your tax return, even if you don't itemize deductions.**

You may deduct as an expense any medicine or drug that is a prescribed drug (determined without regard to whether such drug is available without a prescription) or is insulin. A "prescription" means a written or electronic order for a medicine or drug that meets the legal requirements of a prescription in the state in which the medical expense is incurred and that is issued by an individual who is legally authorized to issue a prescription in that state.

You can only include the medical expenses you paid during the year. Your total deductible medical expenses for the year must be reduced by any reimbursement of deductible medical expenses. It makes no difference if you receive the reimbursement or if it is paid directly to the doctor, hospital, or other medical provider. Any reimbursement from employer, or insurance reduces your medical expense deduction.

Non-deductible items are:

You may not deduct funeral or burial expenses, over-the-counter medicines, toothpaste, toiletries, cosmetics, a trip or program for the general improvement of your health, or most cosmetic surgery (unless

23

it's a result of injury, illness, or physical damage). You may not deduct amounts paid for nicotine gum and nicotine patches, which do not require a prescription.

Important points to remember are:

- Medical, dental, eyecare or healthcare expenses paid (family, self, children or other dependents)

- Diagnostic procedures (body scans, pregnancy tests, and annual physical check-ups)

- Non-prescription equipment and supplies (crutches, braces, blood sugar tests, and walkers)

- Medical conferences and travel to and from (if relating to your chronic disease)

- Gym memberships (If a doctor gives you a prescription for weight loss, rehab, or to correct an injury, illness, or accident. **You cannot already belong to a gym.**)

- Fees paid to Acupuncturists, Chiropractors, and Therapists (if related to a medical condition)

- Medical travel to and from providers (even if accompanied with a care giver)

- Caregivers who aid in home and work (because of a medical condition)

Business owners, partners and shareholders of S-Corporations can deduct health insurance **(incudes Medicare premiums)** on your tax returns

Robert F Hockensmith

WEEK #5 — Little Trick to Write Off Miscellaneous Expenses

When we include our tax deductions, we must always remember the Big Four: Mortgage interest, State income taxes, Real estate taxes and Charitable contributions. John and Edith, a couple starting a business, had this in mind and they were also aware that 2017 was the last year to be able to write off Miscellaneous Expenses on Schedule A.

The Tax Cut and Jobs Act (TCJA) suspends Miscellaneous Expense deductions, but there is still a potential for getting these tax deductions. The couple knows this, because they sought assistance from their tax professional.

If you free-lance, earn side work, or have your own business you can still write off many items that are currently lost for employees. Having your own business allows you to write off any expense that is used for the business. Try to earn non-employee (self-employed) income from free-lance or side work and you can write off many, if not all the expenses listed below.

Internal Revenue Section 162 allows for any expense of operating a business that is reasonable and ordinary. Be sure to check with your state rules, where they might be allowed, too!

Some business deductions are as follows:

- Tax Preparation, Consultation, investment, or planning fees for business

- Advertising, marketing, website creation and maintenance fees

- Auto expenses (be sure to keep a logbook, if you use the vehicle for both business and personal trips) No logbook, No deduction!

- Bank Fees and credit card processing fees

- Communication Expenses (phones, internet, data plans)

- Dues, Professional organizations and groups

- Education to improve your existing knowledge in a business (Not allowed if it prepares you for a new career or job, or a new professional license).

- Equipment purchased or repaired and maintained

- Health insurance premiums (includes Medicare insurance)

- Home Office expenses (you can have more than one office)

- Legal, accounting or other professional fees to manage or defend your income (professional athletes get to deduct fines they pay to their leagues for misconduct.)

- License Fees and renewals

- Office equipment and supplies

- Payroll and sub-contractor expenses

- Printing, postage, and shipping costs

- Travel, transportation and lodging expenses (many expenses here that you wouldn't think of)

- Uniforms and laundry expenses

- Qualified Business Income deduction

- Check with azmoneyguy, or your tax advisor, to see if your situation and circumstances allow you to deduct business expenses.

WEEK #6 – Tax Tips for the Homeowner and Vacation Home Rentals

Who isn't excited about a new home? Whether you are a first-time homeowner like Julie and Sandra or an experienced homeowner, the fun of buying a new home remains unparalleled. And what better news than to learn that buying a home also brings along with it some tax advantages.

This week we'll discuss some tax tips for the homeowner. If you're a first-time homeowner or if you haven't owned a home in the past two years, maybe buying a house, taking out a mortgage, and moving are at the forefront of your mind. If you have owned a home for more than a year, you already know the tax benefits of owning a home. Here are some of the different types of deductions available on your federal tax return because you own a home:

- **Mortgage Interest** - mortgage owed cannot exceed the value of the home. If so, then the excess mortgage is considered Investment Interest, rather than Mortgage Interest. And both mortgage and investment interest deductions are only available up to certain dollar limits. The Tax Cut & Jobs Act (TCJA) rules state, "Mortgage Interest, Home Equity Lines of Credit (HELOC) and second mortgages are only deductible, if the debt is acquisition debt". This means you CAN'T use a mortgage to buy a car, pay off credit cards or for any other

31

reason, and deduct the mortgage interest. **You can only take out a mortgage to buy the home or add to the home and deduct the mortgage interest.** So, if you have a mortgage, HELOC, second mortgage or other type of real estate secured loan, be sure you can prove what the money was used for, when you took out the loan! Mortgage interest is limited to $750,000 mortgage debt.

- **Prepaid mortgage interest** - on original purchase and any refinance of property depending on date of the month you close.

- **Points or Origination Fees** - deductible for points paid up front or at closing, either by you or the seller.

- **Real Estate Taxes** - current or prepaid real estate taxes are deductible, up to certain limits.

- **Mortgage Insurance Premiums** – sometimes these are known as MIP or PMI. (Extended thru 2020)

- **Cancellation of Mortgage Debt** – This is still available for Qualified Mortgage indebtedness up to $2,000,000 of relief. If you are forgiven mortgage debt for your personal residence, you report the debt relief, but you pay NO taxes on this relief. Certain exceptions apply,

- **Capital Gains Exclusion** - on profits of sale of personal residence up to $250,000 for single and $500,000 for married couple, but you must live in the home two (2) of five (5) years, with a few exceptions for military service, change in employment, medical reasons, or other unforeseen circumstances.

Vacation Home Rentals

If you rent a home to others, you usually must report the rental income on your tax return. But you may not have to report the income if the rental period is short and you also use the property as your home. In most cases, you can deduct the costs of renting your property. However, your deduction may be limited, if you also use the property as your home.

Following are some basic tax information that you should know if you rent out a vacation home:

- **Vacation Home Defined**
  A vacation home can be a house, apartment, condominium, mobile home, boat or similar property.

- **Schedule E**

  You usually report rental income and rental expenses on Schedule E, Supplemental Income and Loss.

- **Used as a Home**

  If the property is "used as a home," your rental expense deduction is limited. This means your deduction for rental expenses can't be more than the rent you received. For more about these rules, see Publication 527, Residential Rental Property (Including Rental of Vacation Homes), or speak with a tax professional.

- **Divide Expenses**

  If you personally use your rental property and rent it to others, special rules apply. You must divide your expenses between the rental use and the personal use. To figure how to divide your costs, you must compare the number of days for each type of use with the total days of use.

- **Personal Use**

  Personal use may include use by your family. It may also include use by any other property owners or their family. Use by anyone who pays less than a fair market rental price is also personal use.

- **Schedule A**

  Report deductible expenses for personal use on Schedule A, Itemized Deductions. These may include costs such as mortgage interest, property taxes and casualty losses.

- **Rented Less than 15 Days**

  If the property is "used as a home" and you rent it out fewer than 15 days per year, you do not have to report the rental income. It's TAX FREE, no matter how much you receive!

Also remember to keep receipts, settlement statements, and any other purchase documents, when buying, improving, or refinancing a home, for as long as you own the home, plus seven (7) years. The expenses, or costs, prove your basis (what you paid) for the property. This will reduce or eliminate any taxes owed on profits made when you sell the house. Keep these purchase or home improvement receipts in a safe place, so you will have them to show your tax professional and possibly the IRS; if you are audited or questioned.

Robert F Hockensmith

WEEK #7 – Top Ten Tips to Help You Choose a Tax Professional

Choose wisely, when you intend to get the bang for your buck. Linda and Priscilla are very diligent about getting their money's worth and that explains why they screen cautiously when it comes to choosing a tax preparer. If you pay someone to prepare your income tax return, the IRS urges you to choose that person wisely.

Here are ten tips to keep in mind when choosing a tax preparer:

1. **Check the preparer's qualifications.**

   All paid tax preparers are required to have a Preparer Tax Identification Number or PTIN. In addition to making sure they have a PTIN, ask the preparer if they attend continuing education classes. All licensed tax preparers must attend continuing education, annually. You can see if a tax preparer is licensed with that State Board of Accountancy (CPAs) or is qualified with the IRS (EA) or are members of the state bar (Attorney). The IRS provides links that allow taxpayers (you) the ability to verify whether a tax preparer is an Enrolled Agent (EA). The link is at

   https://irs.treasury.gov/rpo/rpo.jsf

   Each state has a Board of Accountancy to verify Certified Public Accountants (CPA) and a state bar to verify Attorneys.

2. **Check the preparer's history.**

   Check to see if the preparer has a questionable history. Look for disciplinary actions and for the status of their licenses.

3. **Ask about fees.**

   Avoid preparers who base their fee on a percentage of your refund or those who say they can guarantee larger refunds than others can. Always make sure any refund due is sent to you or deposited into your bank account. Taxpayers should **never** deposit their refund into a preparer's bank account. Ask what the estimated fees will be before the tax returns are prepared. Your tax professional should be able to give you a good estimate, so the final bill is not a surprise!

4. **Ask to e-file your return.**

   Make sure your preparer offers IRS e-file. Any paid preparer who prepares and files more than 10 returns for clients generally must file the returns electronically. See week 3 for exceptions.

5. Make sure the preparer is available.

Make sure you'll be able to contact the tax preparer after you file your return - even after the April 15 due date. This may be helpful in the event questions come up during the year.

6. Provide records and receipts.

Good preparers will ask to see your records and receipts. They'll ask questions to determine your total income, deductions, tax credits and other items. Do not use a preparer who is willing to e-file your return using your last pay stub instead of your Form W-2, or substitute Form W-2. This is against IRS e-file rules.

7. Never sign a blank return.

Don't use a tax preparer that asks you to sign a blank or incomplete tax form.

8. Review your return before signing.

Before you sign your tax return, review it and ask questions if something is not clear. Make sure you're comfortable with the accuracy of the return, before you sign it. Remember, you are still legally responsible for what is on it.

9. Ensure the preparer signs and includes their PTIN.

Paid preparers must sign returns and include their PTIN as required by law. The preparer must also give you a copy of the return. If a paid preparer does not sign a return, it is illegal, they can be sanctioned and even lose their licenses, plus face fines, penalties and possibly be barred from preparing future tax returns. NEVER use a preparer that doesn't sign the tax returns they complete!

10. Report abusive tax preparers to the IRS.

You can report abusive tax preparers and suspected tax fraud to the IRS. Use Form 14157, Complaint: Tax Return Preparer. If you suspect a return preparer filed or changed the return without your consent, you should also file Form 14157-A, Return Preparer Fraud or Misconduct Affidavit. You can get these forms at IRS.gov or by calling 800- TAX-FORM (800-829-3676)

WEEK #8 – Property Tax Valuation

Marching through the weeks of the New Year, we step into March. This is the time when winter gradually makes way for spring and while enjoying the beauty of the budding flowers in their garden, Steve and Debra are aware that there is another task awaiting their attention.

Usually each year in March, property owners start receiving annual Property Tax Valuation Notices. These are notices from the County Assessor that inform real property owners how much property tax is owed for each house or piece of real estate. This will be based on the assessed value of the property from last year. Typically, Property Tax Valuations are 18 months behind the current property values.

While the couple know the property valuation notices may reflect some DIFFERENCE from the current value of their real estate, they still need to consider whether they want to appeal the Property Tax Valuation they receive. Sometimes the valuation notice will be lower than your property's current value and sometimes it may be higher. Remember, appealing your valuation notice could either increase or decrease what taxes you owe on your real estate. Steve and Debra know that they must understand all these factors before considering their next options.

To fully comprehend your property taxes, there are some points to understand. The Full Cash Value (FCV) should reflect current market value. Your Limited Property Value (LPV) is the figure that will likely change on your new Valuation Notice. This number is what is used to assess taxes for school districts, cities, community colleges, and counties. It's important to appeal sooner, rather than later.

Each owner has 60 days from the notice date to appeal the property valuation either online or by mail. If you don't think you can sell your property for the Full Cash Value listed, consider appealing. If there is something wrong with the information the County Assessor used to value your home, such as square footage, consider appealing. If you believe bad comparisons or sales of comparable homes ("comps") have been used to assess the value of your home, consider appealing.

Additionally, each piece of real estate is divided into a specific property class such as residential, commercial, raw land, and rental classifications. Each classification determines the rate at which the property will be assessed. For instance, residential property might get (.1) tax rate assessment while a rental property might get a (.3) tax rate assessment, etc.

Often property owners do not let the assessor know when they are renting real estate to others and this can cause real problems with property assessments, since you can only have ONE primary residence at a time, regardless of how many pieces of real estate you own. Frequently County Assessors will send letters to owners of multiple real estate properties asking for clarification of ownership. Not being honest with such inquiries can cause both legal and financial problems for real property owners.

Here are some points to remember:

- Property Tax Assessments come out in March

- Property Tax Valuations are usually 18 months behind the actual market valuations

- Property assessments and tax rates are based upon different property classification (rental, commercial, raw land, primary residence, etc.)

- County Assessors are now sending letters asking owners of multiple properties, which one is the primary residence (only one is allowed at a time)

- Appealing your valuation may increase or decrease the taxes you owe

- **Consider appealing your assessment if:**

  - Full Cash Value (market value) is wrong

  - Your property square footage is wrong

  - Sales of comparable homes are wrong for your neighborhood

- **Remember, when appealing, you are arguing that the assessment is wrong, not arguing that the value of the property is wrong. If you argue the property value is wrong, your appeal will be denied. Be sure to argue one or more of the three (3) consider appealing bullets above.**

WEEK #9 – Non-Cash Charitable Contributions

Being generous counts and can offer donors great tax deductions too. Donating that old treadmill, which has been lying unused for years might reap some tax benefits. Harley and Foster know this, so every year they always keep track of what they are donating and the condition it was in when they donate items.

Most taxpayers donate far more dollar value than they realize, but they seldom keep track of it.

Generally, taxpayers will claim around $500 of non-cash donations, but if they keep track of their non-cash donations, we find families donate closer to $3000 worth. That means about $800 in tax refunds are being lost, every year! This type of deduction could save you hundreds or thousands of dollars each year, but you must document your contributions. Keeping good records is what will always win, in case of an audit.

This week we will discuss non-cash contributions. Non-cash items are furniture, clothing, home appliances, sporting goods, artwork and any item you contribute other than cash, checks, or by credit card.

Generally, you can deduct your cash contributions and the Fair Market Value (FMV) of most property you donate to a qualified charitable organization. Special rules apply to several types of donated property, including clothing or household items, cars, and boats. If your contribution entitles you to receive merchandise, goods, or services in return – such as admission to a charity banquet or a sporting event – you can deduct only the amount that exceeds the FMV of the benefit received. FMV is generally the price you would get, had you sold the property in an open market. Usually the receipt you receive for the donation will state how much that is.

To claim a deduction for donated property valued at $250 or more, you must have a written statement or receipt from the charitable organization. It must show the amount of the donation and a description of the property given. It must also say whether the charity provided any goods or services in exchange for the gift.

If you donate property, the receipt that you are given must include a description of the items and a good faith estimate of its value. For items valued at $500 or more of total non-cash items (food, clothes, electronics, computers, household goods, furniture, etc.) you must complete Form 8283, Non-Cash Charitable Contributions.

If you claim a deduction for a contribution of non-cash property worth $5,000 or more for any one item, generally an appraisal must be obtained, and Section B of Form 8283 must be completed and filed with your return, and you must attach a copy of the written appraisal along with the tax return. If you file electronically, you will attach a PDF of the appraisal to the tax return, otherwise you can send in a written copy of the appraisal when filing a paper tax return.

It's a best practice to take pictures of items donated when giving away Non-Cash items (clothes, furniture, household items, artwork, etc.), because this helps show the condition and the number (#) of the items donated. This way you can better prove your valuation amount used.

The Salvation Army has a website that is used to value items that are given to charitable organizations, by simply going to the website www.salvationarmyusa.org, and type in the word "valuation" in the search bar. You will see different items that are given away and the valuation that has been accepted by the IRS for charitable donation purposes, based on the condition of the item, for each item donated. Additionally, our office has a Non-Cash charity contribution checklist that is available **free to the public** that can be used in preparing your tax returns. If anyone wants a copy of this, simply contact our office, or online at **AZMONEYGUY.COM**

Here are some points to remember:

- Most families donate closer to $3000 worth of non-cash items, but only claim around $500 on their tax returns

- Be sure to get a written receipt for any cash, check or credit card contribution of $250 or more

- Use form 8283 if the amount of total non-cash charity is $500 or more

- Take pictures of items donated, to prove condition and number (#) of items given

- You will need a written appraisal (stating that it is for tax purposes) if the value of the item being donated is $5000 or more, for any one item

- Use Salvation Army website, (www.salvationarmyusa.org) to determine the value of the items donated

- Contact AZMONEYGUY for a Non-Cash donations checklist

WEEK #10 – Retirement Savings Tips and Making IRA Contributions

Who doesn't aspire for peace of mind during the sunset years? Well, everyone does! We all know that to have a good retirement, you must start saving early in life. Bob and Devin know that saving for retirement will not only help them financially for the future but will also direct them towards helping themselves this year too. Disciplined savers will only get closer toward their retirement dream. So, this week let's discuss the Retirement Savings programs that encourage taxpayers to save for the future.

You can boost your retirement savings even more this year, thanks to the higher limits on some of the most popular savings strategies. Stretch your budget to take maximum advantage of these new limits, especially as studies show most of us save way too little.

Here are some retirement savings plans that are available:

- You can defer (save) into your 401k. The deferral or savings also applies to Tax Sheltered Annuities (TSA's) that are available to teachers, and some government workers. The deferral (savings) limit for Simple (Individual Retirement Accounts) IRA's is a different amount from the other IRA plans.

- Catch up contributions (the extra savings that allows taxpayers to save even more) for those of age 50 and over are available for most retirement plans.

- The limit of both retirement savings accounts and catch up amounts might change annually. You can find the amounts allowed at **www.irs.gov**

- There is both a Traditional IRA and ROTH IRA, in addition to other retirement savings plans. The limits for both Roth and Traditional IRAs can be found by going to **www.IRS.gov** or asking your tax professional. Catch up contributions allowed for those 50 and older.

Here are some tips to maximize your retirement savings:

1. Contribute enough to at least obtain your employer's match in a retirement plan.

2. Defer as much income as you can each month. Try to max out the upfront contribution giving you bigger take-home pay later. If you reach the age of 50 during the year, remember to factor in your catch-up contribution for that year as you will be allowed to make extra contributions.

3. Contribute to an IRA as early in the year as possible to maximize savings.

4. You might be entitled to a Retirement Savings Credit, if you contribute to a Retirement Savings Plan. Your tax preparer can help you with that determination. This could lead you to save thousands in taxes.

5. Be sure to contribute to some type of Retirement plan each year in order to plan for retirement. There are many types of plans, so be sure to speak to your tax professional to see which one or ones you are eligible for (401K, Solo 401K, SEP-IRA, Simple-IRA, IRS code section 403B (Tax Sheltered Annuity-TSA), IRS code section 457 plans (Deferred Compensation plan), Federal TSP plan (Thrift Savings Plan), Traditional IRA and ROTH IRA.

Making IRA Contributions

If you made IRA contributions or you're thinking of making them, you may have questions about IRAs and your taxes. Here are some important tips about saving for retirement using an IRA:

1. There is no age limit to contribute to an IRA.

2. You must have taxable compensation to contribute to an IRA. This includes income from wages and salaries and net self-employment income. It also includes tips, commissions, bonuses and alimony. If you're married and file a joint return, generally only one spouse needs to have compensation.

3. You can contribute to an IRA at any time during the year. To count for this year, you must make all contributions by the due date of your tax return. This does NOT include extensions. That means you usually must contribute by April 15th. If you contribute between Jan. 1 and April 15, make sure your plan sponsor applies it to the right year.

4. For example, the most you can contribute to your IRA for 2019 and 2020 is the smaller of either your taxable compensation for the year or $6,000. If you were age 50 or

older at the end of 2019 or 2020, the maximum you can contribute increases to $7,000.

5. You normally won't pay income tax on funds in your traditional IRA until you start taking distributions from it. Qualified distributions from a Roth IRA are tax-free.

6. You may be able to deduct some or all your contributions to your traditional IRA. See your tax professional's instructions to figure the amount that you can deduct. Unlike a traditional IRA, you can't deduct contributions to a Roth IRA.

7. If you contribute to an IRA, you may also qualify for the Saver's Credit. The credit can reduce your taxes by thousands of dollars. Use **Form 8880**, Credit for Qualified Retirement Savings Contributions, to claim the credit.

Inheriting Retirement Accounts (2020 and later)

The new Setting Every Community up for Retirement Enhancement Act (SECURE) changes the way some people will inherit retirement accounts. Before the SECURE Act was passed and signed into law, Dec 29, 2019, you were able to inherit retirement accounts and *stretch* the amount of time you took to receive the money, so you could pay less taxes over time.

NOW, with the new law, that strategy is much reduced for many people who inherit retirement accounts. **New rules require that inherited retirement accounts must be completely distributed to heirs within 10 years of inheriting them!** This means no more stretching out the payments and the resulting taxes from the extra income.

There are some exceptions to this, such as:

- Inherited accounts prior to 2020
- Spouses
- Minor Children
- Disabled or Chronically ill beneficiaries
- Heirs not more than 10 years younger than the deceased

Here are some points to remember when trying to save for retirement, and maybe even reduce your taxes:

- 401K, 403B (TSA), 457 (Deferred Compensation), Thrift Savings Plans (TSP) contribution plans.
- Simple IRA and SEP IRA contribution plans.
- Catch up for Age 50 and older plans.
- Contribute enough to at least obtain your employer's match. (This always gives you free money)

- Consider the Retirement Saver's Credit. (Ask your tax professional if you qualify for a saver's credit to reduce your taxes)

- Find the Annual limits of the retirement savings accounts AND the Catch-Up amounts from your tax professional.

New SECURE act changes how inherited retirement accounts are distributed

WEEK #11 - Itemizing vs. Standard Deduction: Five Tips to Help You Choose

When you start planning early, you have time on your side to help you compare between various options and choose the best for yourself. While filing your tax return, you usually have a choice of whether to itemize deductions or take the standard deduction. Before you choose, it's a good idea to figure your deductions using both methods. Then choose the one that allows you to pay the lower amount of tax. The one that results in the higher deduction amount often gives you the most benefit.

The IRS offers these tips to help you choose:

1. Figure your itemized deductions. Add up deductible expenses you paid during the year. These may include expenses like:

    - Home mortgage interest, up to $750,000 in mortgage debt.

    - State and local income taxes **or** sales taxes (but not both), real estate and personal property taxes, up to $10,000.

- Gifts to charities, (cash and non-cash) up to 60% of your adjusted gross income.

- Casualty or theft losses if in a Federal Declared Disaster.

- Unreimbursed medical, dental, optical expenses and health insurance.

2. Know your standard deduction. If you don't itemize, your basic standard deduction depends on your filing status (each year the numbers change, be sure to know this year's numbers by asking your tax professional).

- Single

- Married Filing Jointly

- Head of Household

- Married Filing Separately

- Qualifying Widow(er) (widows and widowers with minor children)

Your standard deduction is higher if you're 65 or older and/or blind. If someone can claim you as a dependent, that can limit the amount of your standard deduction.

3. Check the exceptions. Some people don't qualify for the standard deduction and therefore should itemize. This includes married couples who file separate returns when one spouse itemizes.

Robert F Hockensmith

WEEK #12 - Tips about Taxable and Nontaxable Income

If there is an income, there usually is a tax on it. Kevin and Melissa understand it very well and that explains their meticulous planning for the year. This week we discuss what type of income must be reported on tax returns. Are you looking for a hard and fast rule about what income is taxable and what income is not taxable? The fact is that all income is taxable, unless the law specifically excludes it.

Taxable income includes money you receive, such as wages, and tips. It can also include noncash income from property or services. For example, both parties in a barter exchange must include the Fair Market Value (FMV) of goods or services received as income on their tax return. And sometimes your Social Security Benefits are subject to tax as well.

Some types of income are NOT TAXABLE except under certain conditions, including:

- Life insurance proceeds paid to you are usually not taxable. But if you redeem a life insurance policy for cash, any amount that is more than the cost of the policy is taxable.

- Income from a qualified scholarship is normally not taxable. This means that amounts you use for certain costs, such as tuition and required books, are not taxable. However, amounts you use for room and board are taxable.

- If you received a state or local income tax refund, the amount may be taxable. You should have received a **Form 1099-G** from the state agency that made the payment to you, if you received a state refund. If you didn't get it by mail, the agency may have provided the form electronically. Contact them to find out how to get the form. Report any state refund you got, even if you did not receive Form 1099-G. You must still report it, even if you are not taxed on it. This is known as the tax benefit rule.

Here are some types of income that are usually NOT TAXABLE:

- Gifts and inheritances

- Child support payments

- Welfare benefits

- Damage awards for physical injury or sickness

- Cash rebates from a dealer or manufacturer for an item you buy
- Reimbursements for qualified adoption expenses

- Alimony payments **(divorces decreed after 2018)**

- Foster Care Payments

Social Security Benefits (Taxable or Not?)

For some taxpayers reaching Social Security age of 62 and older, allows them the opportunity to start receiving benefits. At age 62 you can start receiving benefits early, but there could be some reduction of benefits involved if you are still earning a wage between ages 62-67. Monthly benefits can be paid to a spouse, ex-spouse, children, widow or dependent parents of retired or deceased workers. **Important point, Social Security limits the amount of monthly benefit a family can receive! This may affect when you start taking your benefits.**

You must have 40 quarters (10 years) paying into Social Security in order to be qualified to receive Social Security benefits. These quarters are determined by how much you earned, and how long you worked each year.

If you are earning income and receiving Social Security benefits, you **may** find yourself paying taxes on some of your Social Security benefits. Single taxpayers earning over $25,000 will pay income taxes on some of their social security benefits. Married Filing Joint taxpayers earning over $34,000 will pay income taxes on some of their social security benefits. As much as 85% of your social security benefits can be subject to taxation.

This does not mean that you pay 85% tax; it means that 85% of your benefits could be taxed at whatever your tax bracket is. You have an option of having Federal Income Taxes withheld from your Social Security benefits to help reduce the amount of tax that may be owed at year end. You may have to pay estimated tax payments on a quarterly basis.

Each year the earnings limit changes, so be sure to see Azmoneyguy or another tax professional to see if your Social Security benefits are taxable.

Here are some Social Security points to remember:

- If you take social security benefits before your full retirement age and you still work, you may find the amount of your benefits reduced.

- If you receive Social Security Benefits you may have to pay taxes.

- Remember that you should speak with Azmoneyguy or a tax professional to determine when you should take your social security benefits. Usually, if you are working you should wait until you reach Full Retirement Age (according to Social Security rules). If you are not working, you usually want to take your social security benefits at the earliest age possible. Your tax professional should be consulted before making a financial decision. **You may even be able to take some of your spouse's or former spouse's Social Security benefits!**

- Social Security **limits** the amount of monthly benefit a **family** can receive! Be sure to plan before taking benefits.

Robert F Hockensmith

.

WEEK #13 — Common Tax Filing Mistakes

Here we are at the April tax deadline. But if you have started preparing early like Dave and Julia, then you have enough time left to cross check what you did. This will ensure reduction or elimination of any mistakes in the process. People often make the same mistakes every year, so here are a few last-minute tips to remember:

1. **Miscalculating the basis of investments**

   Using the wrong basis can cause more taxes to be paid than should be. (Basis is what you paid for assets or investments, plus any dividends or capital gains that have been reinvested.)

2. **Failing to deduct health insurance (includes Medicare)**

   Business owners, partners and shareholders in S-Corporations can deduct health insurance or Medicare premiums without itemizing deductions. So, if you take the Standard deduction, you can still deduct health insurance on your tax return.

3. **Overlooking dependency tax deduction or credit breaks**

   Often, taxpayers don't realize that taking care of a relative may offer a tax deduction. (More than 50% of care and support for family member or individual who lives with you, goes to college or lives in a nursing home.)

4. **Failing to apply carryover items from previous years**

   Losses not able to be used in one year can be carried over for many years. (Capital losses, net operating losses, and charitable contributions are some examples.)

5. **File an amended return when you realize you made a mistake**

   If you do not file amended returns, you could lose tax benefits and/or possible refunds. (Will not invite an audit and you have three (3) years from the date you filed the original returns to file an amended return.)

6. **Choosing the wrong filing status**

   Married, Single, or Head of Household status on December 31st is correct status to claim. No matter what your filing status is during the year or part of the year, whatever your status is as of DECEMBER 31, each year IS the filing status for the whole year. There are some exceptions to this, so be sure to ask your tax professional.

7. **Claiming ineligible dependents**

   Cannot claim dependent if already claimed on another person's return.

8. Failing to file a tax return when a refund is due

Some people think they can delay filing tax returns because they believe they are entitled to a refund. Refunds are forfeited three years after the original due date of a tax return.

9. Correctly add your taxes owed

A computer will guarantee this, but if doing your taxes by hand, mistakes can be and are often made.

10. Sign and date the tax returns

If you don't sign and date your returns and send them in, you can be fined or penalized for a frivolous tax return penalty.

11. Send your return to the right address

If you have a refund, your return goes to a different address than if you owe taxes. Don't confuse the address to where you send your returns, or it could delay your refund or the filing of your tax returns.

12. Be sure the social security numbers and names agree

Be sure to write your Social Security Number (SSN) on the returns. Often taxpayers leave out a number or use a wrong SSN, and sometimes mis-spell names on tax returns. This year you may find that tax deductions have been disallowed if the social security numbers and names do not agree. If you have been married or divorced, be sure that your name has been changed with the Social Security Administration to ensure accurate tax return filing.

13. Wrong bank account numbers

You should choose to get your refund by direct deposit. The fastest and safest way to get a tax refund is to combine e-file with direct deposit. But it's important that you use the right bank and account numbers on your return. Always be sure to check before you send in the returns for accuracy.

14. Electronic filing PIN errors

When you e-file, you sign your return electronically with a Personal Identification Number. If you know last year's e-file PIN, you can use that. If not, you'll need to request your prior year's PIN from the IRS. Do this on www.IRS.gov and be sure to enter your Adjusted Gross Income (AGI) from your prior year's return, in order to have the IRS give you last year's PIN.

15. Consider filing an extension of time to file your tax return, with a Form 4868

16. Filing an extension can make a big difference if you owe taxes. If you do not owe taxes, then an extension is not necessary. But if you do owe taxes, and you don't file an extension, the taxes owed could have a five percent (5%) penalty added onto the tax return. Taxes owed with an

extension only have a one-half of one percent (1/2 of 1%) penalty attached to the taxes. That's only 10% of the usual penalty, just by filing an extension!

WEEK #14 – Tax Extensions and Penalties

We have only a few DAYS left before the filing season is over. Extending the due date of filing your returns will let you file up to October 15th this year. BUT it does not give you extra time to pay any taxes owed. Usually Dennis and Karen are diligent about filing their tax returns, and that explains why they prepare early. That way they have time to go through last minute checks and cross-checks to reduce or eliminate any mistakes in the process. But, in case you are unable to meet the deadline, you should know about your options.

We expect to see a lot more taxpayers filing their tax returns late because, if they have their extensions filed and they owe taxes, the penalty for late payment of your taxes, is only one-half of one percent (1/2 of 1%). There is also a penalty for not filing your returns, and another penalty for under payment of taxes.

Many of us are still scrambling to get our taxes together. So, if you are not prepared to file the tax return by the April deadline, what happens if you can't get your taxes done by the due date? If you need more time, you can get an automatic six-month extension from the IRS. You don't have to explain why you're asking for more time, either.

Here are a few important things to know about filing an extension:

1. **File on time even if you can't pay**

   If you complete your tax return, but can't pay the taxes you owe, file your return on time and pay as much as you can. That way you will avoid the late filing penalty, which is higher than the penalty for not paying all the taxes you owe on time. Plus, you do have payment options.

   Apply for a payment plan using the Online Payment Agreement tool on www.IRS.gov .You can also file Form 9465, Installment Agreement Request, with your tax return. If you are unable to make payments because of a financial hardship, the IRS will work with you.

   Filing an extension on time will reduce your tax penalties by a LOT! Late filing penalties go from 5% of the tax owed down to ½ of 1% of the tax owed, with an extension!

2. **Extra time to file is not extra time to pay**

   An extension to file will give you six more months to file your taxes, until Oct. 15. It does not give you extra time to pay your taxes. You still must estimate and pay what you owe by the April deadline (usually April 15th). You will be charged interest on any amount not paid by the deadline. You may also owe a penalty for not paying on time. But filing an extension will reduce the penalty (see #1 above).

3. **Use IRS Free File to request an extension**

You can use IRS Free File to e-file your extension request. Free File is only available through the IRS.gov website, and there are income limitations. You must e- file the request by midnight of the April deadline. If you e-file your extension request, the IRS will acknowledge receipt, via email.

4. **Use Form 4868**

You can also request an extension by mailing a Form 4868, Application for Automatic Extension of Time to File U.S. Individual Income Tax Return. You must submit this form to the IRS by the April due date. Form 4868 is available on **https://www.IRS.gov**. You don't need to submit a paper Form 4868 if you make a payment using an IRS electronic payment option. The IRS will automatically process your extension when you pay electronically. You can pay online or by phone.

5. Electronic funds withdrawal

If you e-file an extension request, you can also pay any balance due by authorizing an electronic funds withdrawal from your checking or savings account. To do this you will need your bank routing and account numbers.

6. Consider Form 1127

You can also request filing IRS form 1127 if there is a financial   hardship that does not allow you to send money in with the extension   or the tax return. This form does **NOT** give a free pass not to pay taxes. The form provides for NOT having to pay penalties and the interest on penalties **IF** you can prove financial hardship. Death, Disability, High Medical Bills, Bankruptcy and Disasters are examples of reasons the IRS will accept financial hardship requests.

Here are some points to consider for this period:

- **Extension Form 4868** (automatic extension of time to file for up to 6 months) The IRS will approve an extension if you file it by the April deadline.

- **Pay taxes by credit card, check, money order or electronic payment**. (Can be paid over the phone or via internet for a fee) Remember that paying by credit card can cost fees from both the IRS AND the credit card company. You might consider a cash advance, deposit into a checking account, and write a check to IRS for taxes owed.

- **Late payment WITH extension is ½ of 1% of any tax that is not paid by due date**. Having an extension allows you to pay the least amount of any underpayment penalty if you have one.

- **Late payment WITHOUT extension is 5% of tax owed** (cheaper to file an extension). Remember that in addition to a penalty for late payment, there is also an interest charged by the IRS that is compounded daily. Therefore, filing an extension is so much better to do.

- **You owe less than $50,000 and can't pay the tax, file form 9465** (IRS will accept the agreement you propose. There is a fee, and the interest is compounded daily). The IRS gives you up to 6 years to pay taxes owed, but you can NOT be late in filing for the next 5 years' returns.

Form 1127 allows you to file and pay taxes late if you have financial hardship, without an extension (severe hardship must be proven.)

Robert F Hockensmith

WEEK #15 — Paying Income Taxes and Estimated Taxes

The tax season is almost ending, and like any other law-abiding, tax-paying citizen of the country, Chris is aware of his options. He knows that there are four ways to pay the personal income taxes. For convenience and efficiency, these are the available options:

1. Never send cash in the mail.

2. You can pay up to $1,000 a day at all nationwide **7-Eleven stores**, for a fee. Contact **https://www.Azmoneyguy.com** or go to **https://www.irs.gov/payments** for further details.

3. If you e-file, you can file and pay in a single step with an electronic funds withdrawal. If you e-file on your own, you can use your tax preparation software to make the withdrawal. If you use a tax professional to e-file, you can ask the preparer to make your tax payment electronically.

4. You can pay taxes electronically any day of the week and anytime of the day. See Azmoneyguy or go to **https:/www./irs.gov/payments** for further details.

5. You can also pay by check or money order. Make your check or money order payable to the "United States Treasury." Be sure to list the social security number and the tax period that the payment is to be applied to. If you do not, then the IRS or State Department of Revenue or Franchise Tax Board can assign the payment to the period they want to, and this could increase penalties and interest if there are other year's taxes owed as well.

6. Pay your taxes in person (most local IRS offices will accept payments from taxpayers in person, but you must schedule an appointment to see them.)

7. Whether you e-file your tax return or file on paper, you can also pay with a credit or debit card. The credit card company that processes your payment will charge a processing fee. And the IRS may charge a convenience fee if you use a credit card to pay income taxes, too.

8. You may be able to deduct the credit or debit card processing fee on next year's return, on income tax returns before 2018. These fees are deductible on business returns. **This includes IRS form Schedule C businesses as well as other business returns!**

9. Be sure to write your name, address and daytime phone number on the front of your payment. Also, write the tax year, form number you are filing and your Social Security number.

10. Complete Form 1040-V, Payment Voucher, and mail it with your tax return and payment to the IRS. Make sure you send it to the address listed on the back of Form 1040-V. This will help the IRS process your payment and post it to your account. You can get the form on IRS.gov.

11. Remember to enclose your payment with your tax return but do not staple it to any tax form.

12. Pay your tax bill monthly if you are not able to pay in full. Enter an installment plan with the Internal Revenue Service. Therefore, if you owe up to $50,000 you will be able to file a form 9465 and inform the IRS as to what date, each month, the tax bill will be paid and what amount. If your payment is completed within six years (72 months) of the beginning date of the plan, the IRS is required to accept the plan under the new Regulations, and they will NOT file a tax lien against you or your property.

However, if more than $50,000 is owed, a form 9465 and a financial statement disclosure form 433A for personal assets and a form 433B if a business is owned is required. If you owe more than $50,000, the

IRS WILL file a tax lien against you, while you are making payments. Each program also charges a setup fee and interest. The interest charged is compounded DAILY, not monthly!

You must also agree to keep current on tax filings and future tax payments for the next 5 years as well.

This plan is for ONE time only. It is not meant to be used for year after year, and the IRS will terminate the plan after you start it, if you do not pay future taxes on time while you have the installment plan in place. This means you will have to start over again and pay the fees again to re-instate the new plan. (Form 9465 allows you six years (72 months) to pay taxes. Both businesses and individuals can set up payment plans.)

1. You can also ask for a SHORT extension of up to 120 days to pay. This short- term extension is available on the IRS website, under the Online Payment Agreement tool. With the extension, there are reduced penalties and interest and no setup fee is required.

2. You can also request an Offer in Compromise (OIC) as a last resort. The OIC is a way to reduce your amount of taxes owed to the IRS. You can't have any unfiled tax returns, to request an OIC. This is a lengthy process with no guarantee that the

OIC will be accepted. Offers in Compromise should be processed and completed by a tax professional.

3. This is not a DIY program! Fees vary among tax professionals, so ask around. Find someone who has successfully completed OIC's before. The IRS will want to know about all your income and expenses from all sources and may not agree on how much you spend for living expenses. If you qualify, the OIC program is a great way to get a fresh start and a clean slate with the IRS.

Congress passed a law that allows the US State Department to deny or revoke your passport if you owe the IRS $50,000 or more, and do not have a written payment agreement in place.

4. Many states allow the same opportunities, (in person payments, mailing checks, payment plans, credit cards, automatic withdrawals from checking or saving accounts and offers in compromise.) Check with your state for local rules.

If you don't have <u>taxes withheld from your pay,</u> or you don't have enough taxes withheld, then you may need to make Estimated Tax Payments for the current year. If you're self-employed, you normally pay your taxes this way.

Here are some tips you should know about Estimated Taxes:

1. You should pay estimated taxes in the current year, if you expect to owe $1,000 or more when you file your federal tax return. Special rules apply to farmers and fishermen.

2. Estimate the amount of income you expect to receive for the year to determine the amount of taxes you may owe. Make sure that you consider any tax deductions and credits that you will be eligible to claim. Life changes during the year, such as a change in marital status or the birth of a child, can affect your taxes.

3. You normally make estimated tax payments four times a year. The dates that apply to most people are April 15, June 16, Sept. 15 and Jan. 15 of next year (for the previous year ended).

4. You may pay online or by phone. You may also pay by check or money order, or by credit or debit card. If you mail your payments to the IRS, use the payment vouchers that come with Form 1040-ES, Estimated Tax for Individuals.

5. You can now pay your estimates in cash (up to $1000 daily), at any 7-Eleven store in the US. Go to

http://www.irs.gov/payments for details.

See Azmoneyguy or another tax professional to find out if you owe estimated taxes.

WEEK #16 – Tax Return Corrections and Tips for next Tax Year

To err is human and errors happen sometimes, especially if you must hurriedly prepare for your tax returns like Charlie. But to Charlie's relief and for many like him, there are some options. So, this week we will discuss how to correct any information that you accidentally omit from or put incorrectly on your tax return.

The rush is over, and your personal tax return is done for another year. Or so you thought right up to the moment you discovered information that you forgot to include. What do you do next? The action you take depends on the type of information you need to correct.

For instance, if you reported all your income on the return you mailed to the IRS, but you realized you forgot to attach a copy of your Wage Statement, or W-2, the answer is, do nothing. Eventually the IRS will ask for the missing form and at that time you can send it in. Other mistakes made are omitting income or deductions, or finding you are eligible for tax credits, in which case you may have to amend your tax return.

As a rule, if the information you omitted increases the tax you owe, the sooner you file, the cheaper it will be, due to penalties and interest.

On the other side, if the correction results in less tax owed, the earlier you file, the sooner you will receive any refund that is due.

Here are the top ten things to know about filing an amended tax return:

1. **Use Form 1040X**, Amended U.S. Individual Income Tax Return, to correct errors on your tax return. You must file an amended return on paper. **It can't be e-filed**. Remember that if you file state income taxes, then filing an amended Federal return requires that an amended State return also needs to be filed.

2. You usually should file an amended tax return if you made an error claiming your filing status, income, deductions or credits on your original return.

3. You normally don't need to file an amended return to correct math errors. The IRS will automatically make those changes for you. Also, do not file an amended return because you forgot to attach tax forms, such as a W-2 or schedule. The IRS will usually send you a request for those.

4. You usually have three years from the date you filed your original tax return to file Form 1040X to claim a refund. You

can file it within two years from the date you paid the tax, if that date is later. That means the last day for most people to file a 2018 claim for a refund is April 15, 2022. See the 1040X instructions for special rules that apply to certain claims.

5. If you are amending more than one tax return, prepare a 1040X for each year. You should mail each year in separate envelopes. Note the tax year of the return you are amending at the top of Form 1040X. Check the form's instructions for where to mail your return.

6. If you use other IRS forms or schedules to make changes, make sure to attach them to your Form 1040X.

7. If you are due for a refund from your original return, wait to receive that refund before filing Form 1040X to claim an additional refund. Amended returns take up to 12 weeks to process. You may spend your original refund while you wait for any additional refund.

8. If you owe more tax, file your Form 1040X and pay the tax as soon as possible. This will reduce any interest and penalties.

9. You can track the status of your amended tax return three weeks after you file with **'Where's My Amended Return?'** This tool is available on IRS.gov or by phone at 866-464-2050. It's available in English and in Spanish. The tool can track the status of an amended return for the current year and up to three years back.

10. To use 'Where's My Amended Return?' enter your taxpayer identification number, which is usually your Social Security number. You will also need your date of birth and zip code. If you have filed amended returns for multiple years, select each year one by one.

Make Plans Now for Next Year's Tax Return

Most people stop thinking about taxes after they file their tax return. But there's no better time to start tax planning than right now. And it's never too early to set up a smart record-keeping system.

Here are six IRS tips to help you start planning for this year's taxes:

1. **Act when life changes occur.**

   Some life events, like a change in marital status, the birth of a child or buying a home, can change the amount of taxes you owe. When such events occur during the year, you may need to change the amount of tax taken out of your pay. To do that, you must file a new Form W-4, Employee's Withholding Allowance Certificate, with your employer. Use the IRS Withholding Calculator on www.IRS.gov to help you fill out the form. If you receive advance payments of the premium tax credit it is important that you report changes in circumstances, such as changes in your income or family size.

2. **Keep records safe.**

   Put your previous tax return and supporting records in a safe place. That way if you ever need to refer to your return, you'll know where to find it. For example, you may need a copy of your return if you apply for a home loan or financial aid. You can also use it as a guide when you do next year's tax return.

3. Stay organized.

Make sure your family puts tax records in the same place during the year. This will avoid a search for misplaced records, come tax time next year.

Create folders using your last year's tax return, looking at the expenses and the income that you recorded just days ago. For instance, Medical expenses, income, charity, interest expense, and taxes should all be categorized in different folders. This way throughout the rest of the year you can simply throw your source documents into these envelopes and be better organized for year-end.

4. Shop for a tax professional.

If you want to hire a tax professional to help you with tax planning, start your search now. Choose a tax preparer wisely. You are responsible for the accuracy of your tax returns, no matter who prepares it. Find a preparer who is licensed and open all year. **Look for a Certified Public Accountant (CPA), Enrolled Agent (EA), or Attorney. These tax professionals are the only ones who can represent you before the IRS!**

5. Think about itemizing.

If you usually claim a standard deduction on your tax return, you may be able to lower your taxes if you itemize deductions instead. A donation to charity could mean some tax savings. See the instructions for Schedule A, Itemized Deductions, for a list of deductions.

6. **Keep up with changes.**

   Subscribe to IRS Tax Tips to get emails about tax law changes, how to save money and much more. You can also get Tips on IRS.gov or IRS2Go, the IRS's mobile app. **And you can sign up for free tax tips from our office at any time, by sending an email to Robert@azmoneyguy.com, or by subscribing to YouTube.com/AZMONEYGUY and on social media as well.**

WEEK #17 — Basis, Capital Gains, and Losses

Now is the time to act smart, so that you can cut down your taxes by ensuring your basis on your investments is correct. Pauline, an entrepreneur who had just invested in her own startup, was aware of this. She knows that following the tricks of the trade now, may help in cutting down on taxes at the end of the financial year. So, here's the lowdown on getting it right; to your benefit.

Did you buy property for your business last year? Did you sell stocks or mutual funds? Did you receive an inheritance? Did someone gift you a car, house, stock, or any asset other than cash? In all these events, your total costs, investment or inheritance in assets is known as basis that can affect your tax return.

For instance, if you purchased a copy machine for your business and began to use it in the year, the amount of depreciation you can deduct depends on your basis. In this case, basis can affect future year returns since depreciation may be spread over the life of the equipment. Sell the copier before it's totally depreciated, and the remaining basis affects the gain or loss you report on your return.

This proves that basis is important, but how do you establish it? The answer depends on the way you acquire the property. For business assets, such as a copy machine, basis is usually what you pay for it, including sales tax and freight. For stocks, the purchase is your cost-plus commissions. Mutual fund purchases can be more difficult to calculate because you report dividends and capital gains, but often dividends and capital gains are simply put back into the mutual fund.

Reinvestments in mutual funds will increase your basis If someone gifts assets to you (not inherited), then your basis, in that asset, is what the donor paid for it. Property you inherit is typically valued at Fair Market Value (FMV), at the date of death, of the donor. This amount, which is reported to you by the personal representative or trustee, of an estate, is the basis you will use when you sell or dispose of the property (like Mom's house or Dad's car or furniture).

The Internal Revenue Service (IRS) has some great points on how to address capital gains and losses. When you sell a 'capital asset,' the sale usually results in a capital gain or loss. A 'capital asset' includes most property you own and use for personal or investment purposes.

Here are 10 facts from the IRS on capital gains and losses:

1. Capital assets include property such as your home or car. They also include investment property such as stocks and bonds.

2. A capital gain or loss is the difference between your basis and the amount you get when you sell an asset. Your basis is usually what you paid for the asset.

3. You must include all capital gains in your income. Since 2013, you may be subject to the Net Investment Income Tax (NIIT). The NIIT applies at a rate of 3.8% to certain net investment income of individuals, estates, and trusts that have income above statutory threshold amounts.

4. You can deduct capital losses on the sale of investment property. You can't deduct losses on the sale of personal-use property, like your house, car, or furniture, etc.

5. Capital gains and losses are either long-term or short-term, depending on how long you held the property. If you held the property for more than one year, your gain or loss is long-term. If you held it for one year or less, the gain or loss is short-term.

6. If your long-term gains are more than your long-term losses, the difference between the two is a net long-term capital gain. If your net long-term capital gain is more than your net short-term capital loss, you have a 'net capital gain'.

7. The tax rates that apply to net capital gains will usually depend on your income. For lower- income individuals, the rate may be zero percent on some or all their net capital gains. In 2013, the maximum net capital gain tax rate increased from 15 to 20 percent, depending on your income. A 25 or 28 percent tax rate can also apply to special types of net capital gains.

8. If your capital losses are more than your capital gains, you can deduct the difference as a loss on your tax return. This type of loss is known as a Net Capital Loss. This Net Capital Loss is limited to $3,000 per year, or $1,500 if you are married and file a separate return.

9. If your total net capital loss is more than the limit you can deduct, you can carry over the excess losses you are not able to deduct to next year's tax return. You will treat those losses as if they happened that year.

10. You must file Form 8949, Sales and Other Dispositions of Capital Assets, with your federal tax return to report your

gains and losses. You also need to file Schedule D, Capital Gains and Losses with your return.

Here are some points to remember:

- Basis is defined in numerous ways. It is either what you paid for assets or what others paid for it, if gifted to you. But basis is stepped up to Fair Market Value, FMV, if inherited.

- Basis is important to determine gain or loss when you sell or dispose of something

- The higher your basis, the lower your capital gain (thus the lower your taxes)

- Mutual fund basis increases as capital gains and dividends are reported if they are reinvested (add each year to your mutual fund cost). Now, brokerage houses keep this information for you, even if you transfer or move your investments to another brokerage firm.

- Reduce your capital gains tax by keeping track of your basis. Keep an annual log of what you pay for something plus what you reinvest. If you are gifted or inherit assets, then get a basis value from either the estate or the one who gifted it to you.

WEEK #18 —Deductions allowed when you do not itemize

There are lines and then there are fine lines that can be read to understand better about the available options for deductions on tax returns. Shaun and Penny, a married couple and parents of two children, wanted to make the most of the available options. They are aware that there are other tax deductions you can also deduct, in addition to the standard deductions. So, this week we will discuss deductions that are available to be used on your tax return, even if you **DO NOT** itemize.

There are two ways to reduce your income on your income tax returns. Reducing your income is a way to also reduce the income tax you may be responsible for. The two methods are known as *itemizing* your deductions and using the standard deduction. Many taxpayers find that they are better off using the standard deduction, rather than itemizing on their tax returns. The standard deduction is a pre-arranged tax deduction the IRS allows taxpayers to claim on their tax returns, based on marital status, among other things.

For instance, the standard deduction for 2019 for single taxpayers is $12,200, head of household taxpayers can use $18,350, while married filing joint taxpayers are allowed $24,400 as a standard deduction.

This is a reduction of taxable income, before federal income tax is computed.

But some deductions are available without having to itemize and are called deductions FOR Adjusted Gross Income (AGI). Deductions for AGI are ALWAYS better than deductions from AGI (which is either a Standard Deduction or Itemized Deductions).

There are other tax deductions you can also deduct in addition to the standard deductions, for example:

- IRA contributions (There are certain rules allowing this deduction, depending on whether you or your spouse are in a retirement plan at work, and depending on how much income you earn)

- Self-Employment Retirement Savings Plans (SEP, Keogh, SIMPLE)

- Student loan interest

- Tuition fees

- Self-Employment Health Insurance Payments (You can deduct 100% of health insurance premiums and part of any long-term care policy premiums, includes Medicare insurance) For Business owners, partners or shareholders of S-Corporations

- Alimony paid to former spouse **(not allowed for divorces decreed after 2018)**

- Health Savings Accounts (This is a medical savings plan where you can contribute money for future medical bills and get a tax deduction for doing so)

- Self-Employment Social Security and Medicare Tax (Self-employed must pay 100% of any Medicare and Social Security tax to the IRS, but they also receive a ½ deduction on the front of their tax return as a benefit of being self-employed)

- Moving expenses paid because of change in jobs (if member of the military).

- Early withdrawal penalties from CD's, savings accounts, insurance contracts

- Educator expenses for supplies purchased for classrooms

- National Guard or Reservist expenses (for those who work out of town overnight)

- Many of these For AGI deductions have limits. Be sure to ask Azmoneyguy or your tax professional what the limits are for this year.

WEEK #19 – Tips for Farmers and Farm Tax Returns

Bringing food to the plate matters. So those who toil hard to cultivate, grow and harvest this food, for the people, get some great tax benefits. Farmers like Greg and Beverly, who work hard on their farms to produce fresh food are entitled to some benefits. In fact, there are many tax benefits for people like Greg and Beverly, who are in the farming business. Farms include plantations, ranches, ranges and orchards, just to name a few. Farmers may raise livestock, poultry or fish, or grow fruits, trees, plants or vegetables.

Here are 10 things the IRS lists about farm income and expenses to help at tax time:

1. **Crop insurance proceeds.**
   Insurance payments from crop damage count as income. Generally, you should report these payments in the year you get them.

2. **Deductible farm expenses.**
   Farmers can deduct ordinary and necessary expenses they paid for their business. An ordinary expense is a common and

accepted cost for that type of business. A necessary expense means a cost that is appropriate for that business.

3. **Employees and hired help.**

   You can deduct reasonable wages you paid to your full and part-time workers in the farm. You must withhold Social Security, Medicare and income taxes from their wages.

4. **Sale of items purchased for resale.**

   If you sold livestock or items that you bought for resale, you must report the sale. Your profit or loss is the difference between your selling price and your basis in the item. Basis is usually the cost of the item. Your cost may also include other amounts you paid such as sales tax and freight.

5. **Repayment of loans.**

   You can only deduct the interest you paid on a loan if the loan is used for your farming business. You can't deduct interest you paid on a loan that you used for personal expenses.

6. **Weather-related sales.**

   Bad weather such as a drought or flood may force you to sell more livestock than you normally would in a year. If so, you may be able to delay reporting a gain from the sale of the extra animals.

7. **Net operating losses.**

   If your expenses are more than income for the year, you may have a net operating loss. You can carry that loss over to other years and deduct it. You may get a refund of part or all the income tax you paid in prior years. You may also be able to lower your tax in future years.

8. **Farm income averaging.**

   You may be able to average some or all the current year's farm income by spreading it out over the past three years. This may lower your taxes if your farm income is high in the current year and low in one or more of the past three years. Farmers are the only ones allowed to average their income now.

9. **Fuel and road use.**

   You may be able to claim a tax credit or refund of excise taxes you paid on fuel used on your farm for farming purposes.

10. **Qualified Business Income Deduction.**

    The IRS gives you a deduction up to 20% of your profits just for being a business owner. Also, if you are a farmer or rancher forced to sell your livestock because of drought, flood, hurricane or other natural disaster, special IRS tax relief may help you.

For example, the IRS has extended the time to replace livestock that their owners were forced to sell due to drought. If you're eligible, this may help you defer tax on any gains you got from the forced sales. The relief applies to all or part of the states and Puerto Rico affected by the drought. The IRS has a list of which areas are affected on its website, **www.irs.gov/**

Here are several points, the IRS points out from their own tips that you should know about this relief:

- **Defer Tax on Drought Sales.**
  If the drought caused you to sell more livestock than usual, you may be able to defer tax on the extra gains from those sales.

- **Replacement Period.**
  You generally must replace the livestock within a four- year period to postpone the tax. The IRS can extend that period if the drought continues.

- **IRS Grants More Time.**

  The IRS has added one more year to the replacement period for eligible farmers and ranchers. The one-year extension of time generally applies to certain sales due to drought.

- **Livestock Sales that Apply.**

  If you are eligible, your gains on sales of livestock that you held for draft, dairy or breeding purposes apply.

- **Livestock Sales that Do Not Apply.**

  Sales of other livestock, such as those you raised for slaughter or held for sporting purposes and poultry, are **not** eligible for this type of relief.

- **Areas Eligible for Relief.**

  Check out IRS.gov to see which areas are currently affected.

WEEK #20 – Eight Facts about Penalties for Filing and Paying Late and How to Abate (remove) Penalties

Prevention is better than cure, but if circumstances prevent precaution, then here's what you should know. April 15 is the Tax Day deadline for most people. If you're due a refund, there's no penalty if you file a late tax return. But if you owe taxes and you fail to file and pay on time, you'll usually owe interest and penalties on the taxes you pay late. But there are options available to mitigate the effect.

Here are eight facts the IRS explains that you should know about these penalties:

1. If you file late and owe federal taxes, two penalties may apply. The first is a failure-to- file penalty for late filing. The second is a failure-to-pay penalty for paying late.

2. The failure-to-file penalty is usually much more than the failure-to-pay penalty. In most cases, it's much more, so if you can't pay what you owe by the due date, you should still file your tax return on time and pay as much as you can. You should try other **options to pay**, such as getting a loan or

paying by credit card. The IRS will work with you to help you resolve your tax debt. Most people can set up a payment plan with the IRS using the **Online Payment Agreement tool** on IRS.gov.

3. The failure-to-file penalty is normally 5% percent (.05) of the unpaid taxes for each month or part of a month that a tax return is late. It will not exceed 25 percent of your unpaid taxes.

4. If you file your return more than 60 days after the due date or extended due date, the minimum penalty for late filing is the smaller of $135 or 100 percent of the unpaid tax.

5. The failure-to-pay penalty is generally 5% percent (.05) per month of your unpaid taxes. It applies for each month or part of a month your taxes remain unpaid and starts accruing the day after taxes are due. It can build up to as much as 25 percent of your unpaid taxes.

6. If the 5 % failure-to-file penalty and the 5% failure-to-pay penalty both apply in any month, the maximum penalty amount charged for that month is 5 percent (.05).

7. If you requested an extension of time to file your income tax return by the tax due date and paid at least 90 percent of the taxes, you owe; you may not face a failure-to-pay penalty. However, you must pay the remaining balance by the extended due date. <u>You will owe interest on any taxes you pay after the April 15 due date, even if you filed an extension.</u>

8. You will not have to pay a failure-to-file or failure-to-pay penalty if you can show reasonable cause for not filing or paying on time.

IRS Penalty Abatement Procedures

Taxpayers are often unaware that if they are late filing or paying for their tax return, and it causes penalties, they may be able to get out of paying them. If you have demonstrated full compliance (meaning that you have filed your tax returns and paid any tax that was owed) over the past three (3) years, you are then able to request for a waiver of the penalties.

The waiver is called **"First Time Abatement"** (FTA), Internal Revenue Manual (IRM 20.1.1.3.6.1 (11-25-2011)) tells us this is IRS policy and is used to reward past tax-compliant taxpayers and to promote future compliance.

The Inspector General for Tax Administration (TIGTA) found that many taxpayers with compliant (good) tax histories have not been offered, and do not receive, the FTA waiver, from the IRS. So, if you receive a penalty from the Internal Revenue Service (IRS) and you have been in full compliance for the past three years, you should send a certified letter to the IRS requesting abatement of (Failure to File – FTF), (Failure to Deposit – FTD for businesses who pay payroll taxes or company estimated taxes) or (Failure to Pay - FTP) penalties, whichever applies in your situation. These abatement requests are approved if you meet the "clean" past 3-year rule.

This report shows that over 1.2 million taxpayers with Failure to Pay Penalties alone did not receive penalty relief, even though they were qualified for the FTA waiver. So, you must be sure to send in a letter requesting the abatement, it will not be automatically offered to you.

Remember, the IRS does not automatically try to help you out of trouble with taxes. You must exercise and demand your rights. Those that sleep on their rights (meaning – those that do nothing), lose them.

Additionally, you should check with your state Franchise Tax Board or Department of Revenue to see if they have a similar procedure or policy. Always consult with a tax professional before you pay any tax or penalties. Tax professionals can save you more than they charge, in money, time, and peace of mind!

WEEK #21 - Ten Things to Know about IRS Notices and Letters

You've got mail! But this time it's from the IRS. Always remember, there's no need to press the panic button on seeing this. Each year, the IRS sends millions of notices and letters to taxpayers for a variety of reasons. And the important thing to reiterate here is that the IRS always sends letters or notices through mail. **They will not reach out to you through social media or a phone call!** So, beware and never give out your personal details to anyone, who poses to be from the IRS on social media or over the phone. Brenda is aware of this because she called her tax professional, when she received her IRS notice.

Here are ten things to know in case some letter or notice from the IRS shows up in your mailbox:

1. Don't panic. You often only need to respond to take care of a notice. An IRS notice could be either bad news or good news. You never know until you read it. The IRS often will contact by mail to inform you that you have money coming back or a refund due to you, as often as they might say you owe more tax.

2. There are many reasons why the IRS may send a letter or notice. It typically is about a specific issue on your federal tax return or tax account. A notice may tell you about changes to your account or ask you for more information. It could also tell you that you must make a payment.

3. Each notice has specific instructions about what you need to do.

4. You may get a notice that states the IRS has made a change or correction to your tax return. If you do, review the information and compare it with your original return.

5. If you **agree** with the notice, **you usually don't need to reply unless it gives you other instructions or you need to make a payment.** If you are due additional money, the notice will say so, and then you only must wait for the check in the mail. The wait time differs depending upon the reason for the change. If the IRS takes more than 90 days to pay you, you are also entitled to interest being paid to you on the refund amount.

6. If you **do not agree** with the notice, **it's important for you to respond.** You should write a letter to explain why you disagree. Include any information and documents you want

the IRS to consider. Mail your reply with the bottom tear-off portion of the notice. Send it to the address shown in the upper left-hand corner of the notice. Allow at least 30 days for a response. If you wish to have a tax professional speak or represent you, this is where you would tell the IRS who will speak for you. There is a place to list your representative's name, address and phone number, if the IRS needs to contact them.

7. You shouldn't have to call or visit an IRS office for most notices. If you do have questions, call the phone number in the upper right-hand corner of the notice. Have a copy of your tax return and the notice with you when you call. This will help the IRS answer your questions. If you are not comfortable speaking with the IRS, engage or hire a tax professional to speak on your behalf. Tax professionals such as Certified Public Accountants, Enrolled Agents and Attorneys do this for a living. We know what to say and how to speak to the IRS. There is no need for you, the taxpayer to stress out, and become anxious when dealing with the IRS. Let the professional handle these types of communications.

8. Keep copies of any notices you receive with your other tax records.

9. The IRS sends letters and notices by mail. **They do not contact people by email or social media to ask for personal or financial information.** Always be sure to send ALL correspondence to the IRS by certified mail, return receipt required.

10. For more on this topic visit **https://www.IRS.gov/** or see **Publication 594**, The IRS Collection Process. Be sure to contact Azmoneyguy or your tax professional. **DO NOT** try to handle this yourself. Remember, as an old saying goes, "the attorney who represents themselves, has a fool for a client".

WEEK #22 – Fear of Filing Tax Returns and Unclaimed Tax Refunds

Organizing documents, keeping them in order, backtracking on your investments and expenses and all the paperwork involved might sound overwhelming to some. So, they try to escape the whole process of filing tax returns, by simply ignoring the preparation or submission. It's been a month since the filing deadline and most people have already received their tax refunds, while others on extension have yet to file their returns for last year.

Believe it or not there are still some people that have not filed for past years and don't plan on filing their tax returns merely because they are afraid of filing their tax returns. Many taxpayers do not know if they are due refunds or owe taxes, or they believe they owe taxes and therefore decide not to file or do anything about filing.

There are ways to conquer this fear of filing and reduce or abate penalties that may be charged against you. You must remember that the statute of limitations (the time the IRS can chase after you) is 3 years, but only IF you file a return. **The statute does not START, until you file your tax returns.**

The IRS now also gives you an opportunity to pay your taxes over time or even receive interest if a refund is due for you. But if you do not file a tax return within 3 years of when it's due, and you are entitled to a refund, **the IRS will just keep it!** This is just another reason to file your returns.

So, let's look at some points to remember:

- **Collect all expense and tax information, schedule an appointment with azmoneyguy or your tax professional and ASK THE PROFESSIONAL to help you sort through your information and prepare the returns.**

- **Filing a tax return that's due a refund, protects the refund to you (you must file within 3 years of due date), even if the IRS takes a long time to refund you. Plus, the IRS pays you interest on refunds due.**

- **Filing sooner reduces penalties (penalties for failure to file on time can be as high as 25% of the tax owed). PLUS, INTEREST!**

- **You can file a tax return even if you don't have all the facts (you can always go back and amend the tax return for up to 3 years after the original filing, once you get all the relevant information).**

- **You can pay your taxes over time with the IRS if what you owe them is less than $50,000, using form 9465, Tax Installment Payment Agreement.**

Here are the facts you need to know about unclaimed refunds:

- The unclaimed refunds apply to people who did not file a federal income tax return. The IRS estimates that half the potential refunds are more than $1595 per return.

- Some people, such as students and part-time workers, may not have filed because they had too little income to require filing a tax return. They may have a refund waiting if they had taxes withheld from their wages or made quarterly estimated payments. A refund could also apply if they qualify for certain tax credits, such as the Earned Income Tax Credit.

- If you didn't file a return, the law generally provides a three-year window of the original due date to claim a refund from that year. For 2019 returns, the window closes on April 15, 2023.

- The law requires that you properly address, mail and postmark your tax return by that date to claim your refund. We always suggest when mailing returns, do so, certified mail, return receipt requested. Also remember you can e-file your past returns from 2012 tax years forward. AND be sure to use the correct address to send returns in, which is different from the address you send payments in. Your tax professional can help with the correct address or you can go to **www.irs.gov** and find the correct address to mail in returns or payments, based upon where you live.

- If you don't file a claim for a refund within three years, the money becomes property of the U.S. Treasury. There is no penalty for filing a late return if you are due a refund.

- The IRS may delay your 2019 refund if you have not filed tax returns for 2017 and 2018. The U.S. Treasury will apply the refund to any federal or state tax owed. It also may use your refund to offset unpaid child support or past due federal debts such as delinquent student loans.

- If you're missing Forms W-2, 1098, 1095, 1099 or 5498 for prior years, you should ask for copies from your employer, bank or other payer. If you can't get copies, **get a free transcript** showing that information by going to IRS.gov. You can also file **Form 4506-T** to get a transcript.

- The three-year window also usually applies to a refund from an amended return. In general, you must file **Form 1040X**, Amended U.S. Individual Income Tax Return, within three years from the date you filed your original tax return. You can also file it within two years from the date you paid the tax, if that date is later than the three- year rule. This would mean the deadline for most people to amend their 2018 tax return and claim a refund will expire on April 15, 2022.

Robert F Hockensmith

WEEK #23 — High School Students, College Students, Graduates and Taxes

The summer internship with a financial institution of his choice has given wings to Jacob's aspirations. He feels as if his career graph is on the runway to success, all set to take off just the way he wanted it to be. Many students like Jacob, take a job in the summer after school lets out.

If it's your **first job** it gives you a chance to learn about the working world. That includes taxes we pay to support the place where we live, our state and our nation.

Here are eight things that students who take a summer job should know about taxes:

1. Don't be surprised when your employer withholds taxes from your paychecks. That's how you pay your taxes when you're an employee. If you're self-employed, you may have to pay estimated taxes directly to the IRS on certain dates during the year. This is how our pay-as-you- go tax system works.

2. As a new employee, you'll need to fill out a **Form W-4**, Employee's Withholding Allowance Certificate. Your employer will use it to figure how much federal income tax to

withhold from your pay. The **IRS Withholding Calculator** tool on IRS.gov can help you fill out the form.

3. Keep in mind that all tip income is taxable. If you get tips, you must keep a daily log so you can report them. You must report $20 or more in cash tips in any one month to your employer. And you must report all your yearly tips on your tax return.

4. Money you earn doing work for others is taxable. Some work you do may count as self- employment. This can include jobs like baby-sitting and lawn mowing. Keep good records of expenses related to your work. You may be able to deduct (subtract) those costs from your income on your tax return. A deduction may help lower your taxes.

5. If you're in ROTC, your active duty pays, such as pay you get for summer camp, is taxable. A subsistence allowance you get while in advanced training isn't taxable.

6. You may not earn enough from your summer job to owe income tax. But your employer usually must withhold Social Security and Medicare taxes from your pay. If you're self-employed, you may have to pay them yourself. They count toward your coverage under the Social Security system.

7. If you're a newspaper carrier or distributor, special rules apply. If you meet certain conditions, you're considered self-employed. If you don't meet those conditions and are under age 18, you are usually exempt from Social Security and Medicare taxes.

8. You may not earn enough money from your summer job to be required to file a tax return. Even if that's true, you may still want to file. For example, if your employer withheld income tax from your pay, you'll have to file a return to get your taxes refunded.

GRADUATES and TAXES:

Just a reminder for new graduates as you step out of college life, into the work environment and the rest of your life. Here are some tax tips:

- **Student Loan Interest** (you get an "above the line" deduction for up to $2,500 depending on income levels).

- **Student Loan Repayments** (You can now repay up to $10,000 in student loans and interest, from distributions of a 529 Education plan, TAX FREE).

- **Tuition and fees** (you could get a tax deduction or tax credit depending on the type of education and tax deduction you take).

- **Education credits** (Lifetime learning credit available up to a limit, based on income, for education that leads to a college degree or vocational diploma, no matter how old you are and no matter how many other degrees you may already have).

- **Withholding** (be sure when you start a new job you fill out the W-4 form to determine the correct amount of taxes, this may require help from an accountant). See item #2 before. Don't forget to include your state tax withholding too.

- **Retirement Savings Contribution Credit** (people starting a new job or beginning to save with a retirement plan even an Individual retirement plan (IRA) can receive a tax credit for up to $2,000 by starting a 401k or IRA retirement plan not contributed to in the last two years).

Each of these choices has limitations based on the income you earn, and whether you are claiming yourself as an exemption or not. Many times, the first year out of college, the parents still claim the graduate child as a dependent. You must make sure you communicate with your parents, to not double claim exemptions, because that is NOT allowed. Usually, the one earning the most money receives a better tax benefit from claiming you as an exemption. Be sure to ask azmoneyguy or your tax professional which is best for your circumstances.

WEEK #24 – Weddings, Marriage and Taxes

It's that time of the year when many people walk down the aisle and vow to be together till "death do us part". Both Don and Jan are excited about the upcoming event of their lives! While wedding bells ring in happiness and bliss, it also ushers tax worries among other concerns. Summertime is the most traditional time of year for weddings. They paid a visit to their tax professional and were instructed on what to do next.

Although we usually associate marriage with Love, Roses and Cake: If you're walking down the aisle here is a checklist of **TAX** matters to consider:

- **Make sure you change your name with Social Security Administration.**
  This can be done either online or in person. The Social Security Administration is better staffed, and much faster than ever before. If you go in person, you will probably be out very quickly. We dread going to any government office, but this one is on our side.

- **If you move, be sure to change your address formally.**
  (IRS, financial institutions you have accounts with, and your

employer for W2's. File Form 8822, with the IRS. This lets them know your new address, so any refunds or notices will not be delayed).

Each company or government agency you do business with needs to know your new address in writing to be effective. A phone call does not guarantee the update will occur. Be sure to ALWAYS send such mail certified, so it can be tracked and proven that you notified them.

- **Your marital status, as of the last day of the year, will determine your tax filing status.**

No matter what day you are married or divorced, your status as of December 31, each year is your tax status. Once you are either married or divorced be sure to calculate the impact of any marriage penalty to see whether you need to change your income tax withholdings with your W4. (Remember if you divorce, you lose at least one tax benefit, maybe more if your former spouse takes the children; and this will cost you more taxes at year end.)

- **Changes in circumstances.**

The IRS reminds newlyweds to add a health insurance review to their to-do list. This is particularly important if you receive premium assistance through advance payments of the premium tax credit via a Health Insurance Provider or

Marketplace. If you, your spouse or a dependent gets health insurance coverage through the Marketplace, you need to let the Marketplace know you got married. Informing the Marketplace about changes in circumstances, such as marriage or divorce, allows the Provider or Marketplace to help make sure you have the right coverage for you and your family and adjust the amount of advance credit payments that the government sends to your health insurer. Reporting the changes will help you avoid having too much or not enough premium assistance paid to reduce your monthly health insurance premiums. Getting too much premium assistance means you may owe additional money or get a smaller refund when you file your taxes. Getting too little could mean missing out on monthly premium assistance that you deserve. You should also check whether getting married affects your, your spouse's, or your dependents' eligibility for coverage through your employer or your spouse's employer, because that will affect your eligibility for the premium tax credit.

Other changes in circumstances that you should report to the Health Provider or Marketplace include:

- The birth or adoption of a child,

- Divorce,

- Getting or losing a job,

- Moving to a new address, gaining or losing eligibility for employer or government sponsored health care coverage, and

- Any other changes that might affect family composition, family size, income or your enrollment.

In addition, certain life events – like marriage – give you and your spouse the opportunity to sign up for health care during a special enrollment period. That means if one or both of you is uninsured, you may be able to get coverage now. In most cases, the special enrollment period for Marketplace coverage is open for 60 days from the date of the life event.

- **Update your Will and other Estate planning documents annually.**
  IRA's, insurance policies and 401k's all need to be reviewed and/or updated to reflect who the new beneficiary will be, now that your spouse is no longer the primary beneficiary in case something happens to you.

- **Credit scores ALWAYS remain single.**

Did you know that once you are married, your individual credit file and your credit score remain yours alone? Newly married couples may finance a home, a car and other household items as a unit. This fact can confuse the issue, as it lends people to think that they now have a joint credit file and joint credit score. That is not the case. When you apply for credit as co-applicants, both credit files are pulled and considered by the lender. Given that a couple's personal credit is dictated by two individual credit files, it is important to order free credit reports for both yourself and your spouse, and to provide identity protection for both.

- **Tax worries of a new spouse do not have to become problems of the other new spouse.**

  Be sure to consult with a tax professional before you marry. There may be tax issues from a former life or marriage that can haunt you in the new marriage. But there are also ways to make sure that the new marriage is NOT haunted from problems of the past. (Consider filing an Injured Spouse Form 8379).

- **Same sex married couples.**

  If you are legally married in a state or country that recognizes same-sex marriage, you generally must file as married on your federal tax return. This is true even if you and your spouse later live in a state or country that does not recognize same-sex marriage. Be sure you know the rules for the state you live in. It may be the same or different from the Federal tax rules on how to report your taxes.

WEEK #25 – Estate Taxes, Planning and Inheriting Property

Once you are done dealing with a behemoth of paperwork, and tax season is over, it is time to look ahead to ensure a better tax year in the future. With the tax season behind us, now is the perfect time to consider your estate plan.

I read this article in a legal journal and HAD to share it.

What Do You Have in Common with Tony Soprano?

By Michael L. Ferrin | April 17, 2014

James Gandolfini, the actor who played Tony Soprano in the popular television series 'The Sopranos', died of a heart attack while on vacation in Italy. Since then, countless articles have been written by estate planning attorneys and others analyzing, criticizing, and dissecting the lessons to be learned from his estate plan. Most people do not have a potential $30 million estate tax bill due to poor estate planning (which could be seen by some as a nice problem to have), but many of the other problems with Mr. Gandolfini's estate plan are common in most estate plans.

Mr. Gandolfini's personal choices, as well as his estate and tax planning choices have been widely criticized. For example, it is reported that he left the bulk of his estate to his children, sisters and friends rather than his spouse. By holding the assets in trust for the benefit of his wife under an ascertainable standard and then having the balance go to the children on her death, he could have saved significant estate taxes. Perhaps even more problematic is that the children receive their inheritance at age 21. His 9-month old daughter will receive 20% of what is estimated to be a $70 million estate outright at age 21. Using a simple trust, this inheritance could have been protected and managed for her throughout her lifetime, where it would be protected from creditors, shysters, con-men, divorce, and from poor choices that are inevitable when a young person is handed a pile of money before she is adequately prepared to handle it.

Mr. Gandolfini owned real property in Italy. Real property in multiple states and foreign countries can result in multiple costly probates if not properly addressed in an estate plan. Some of his property was vacation property. Vacation properties such as condos and family cabins have unique issues that need to be addressed before they are passed to the next generation. Failure to plan can result in loss of the property or hard feelings between family members.

How does the world know so much about Mr. Gandolfini's estate plan? It really isn't any of our business, is it? The answer is simple. Mr. Gandolfini chose to use a Will rather than a trust. A prominent estate planning attorney stated it this way; *"But, the hardest choice to understand is Gandolfini's choice to use a Will rather than a trust as his primary estate planning vehicle. By using a Will, he subjected his estate to the process of probate. Probate delays and expense vary by jurisdiction. But, in all jurisdictions, probate is a public proceeding. It is difficult to understand why he would choose to air his finances and personal choices in public. It is even more difficult to understand why he would expose his family to this. If he had used a trust rather than a Will, we would not know to whom he had left his fortune."* Steven Hartnett, Associate Director, American Academy of Estate Planning Attorneys.

This type of bombshell happens all the time, because people tend to put off important matters until later. This also happened to Prince, Aretha Franklin, Michael Jackson, Bob Marley, Sonny Bono, and many more!

Perhaps the most important lesson to learn from this is applicable to all of us – don't procrastinate. Mr. Gandolfini died at age 51 while on vacation. He probably assumed he had many good years ahead of him to get his planning in place. It is human nature to put off setting up a trust or updating an estate plan, but this can result in unfortunate situations and problems for the loved ones we leave behind.

Now is the time to consider your estate plans:

- **No estate plan? Establish one ASAP!**
  If you do not create an estate plan, the State where you reside determines allocation of inheritance. This can be a problem if there are children from a current or prior marriage. A Will or

Trust sets the rules of who will inherit what, and who will take of whom in the event of a death or disaster.

- **Do not ignore estate planning just because your estate is under the estate tax threshold.**

  The rules for estate exemption vary year to year, and depends on which state you reside in. Many people feel that if they don't have many assets, there is no need to set up an estate plan. But that is FAR from true! Have a plan in place and review and update annually. Things such as financial situation or heirs could change.

- **Create Will or Trust.**

  This document can specify heirs, allocation of assets, denote representative or guardian of you and/or your minor children. Each one has advantages and disadvantages. There is NOT a one size fits all answer to which is best for each person or family. There are many reasons to consider which works best: Privacy, timing or inheritances, costs, maintaining family harmony, financial position for minors, protecting step family members, asset protection, probate avoidance are but a few of the many issues that can be addressed by choosing the appropriate estate planning vehicle (Will or Trust).

- **Medical POA and/or Living Will**

Provides for your wishes to be carried out if you cannot communicate them at the time.

- **Legal and Financial POA's**

  Gives permission to those you trust to carry out your desires if you cannot communicate with them at the time.

- **Updated Beneficiary designation for Insurance and Retirement Assets**

  Ensures heirs receive monies quickly, without hassle or delay. **(Must change after divorce)**

Here are a few things to keep in mind when discussing a Trust:

1. Some Trusts state that upon the death of either one of you, your assets are to be placed into two separate Trusts. This is typical of most A/B Trusts, Living Trusts, Revocable Trusts, and Family Trusts. This means that when one of you passes there is an A Trust and a B Trust established. The A Trust is the Survivor's Trust and the B Trust is the Decedent's Trust. Frequently people believe if they have a small estate and if there are children or grandchildren involved, they do not have to worry about creating two separate trusts upon the death of their spouse; even though the Trust documents state this should be done. It is my advice and recommendation that you DO create two separate trusts if your trust language tells you

to do so. Especially so with second marriages and blended families.

2. There is a federal estate tax exemption in place if a Trust currently exceeds $11.4 million. (The amount could change each year, contact our office for current exemption amounts). When a person passes, they can shift their unused estate exemption to their spouse. That spouse will have the ability to shelter over $22.8 million (be sure to find out the current exemption amount for this year by calling our office), to not pay taxes for their estate or by allowing their heirs to inherit money tax free. We encourage that an Estate Tax Return be prepared when a spouse passes, regardless of the size of their estate. Wealthy clients understand the need for preparing these returns while the "average" family does not feel that since they do not have a large estate, they do not need to file the return. This omission can impact tax issues with a subsequent marriage, if that results in marrying into a large estate.

3. Make sure your Trust review is less than 5 years old. If you do not have a Trust in place, I strongly recommend having one created, especially if you are married, own a home, or have children. A trust is a great way to keep the transfer of assets private, to prevent family feuds, and to allow for assets

to be transferred quickly at no cost, among other reasons. The cost of preparing a Trust may also be a tax deduction.

Property and Assets

Some taxpayers believe that when they are older it is safer to have their beneficiaries or heirs listed as joint owners on their property, checking accounts, savings accounts, automobiles and houses. The parents think they are doing the children a favor and making things easier by having their children named as joint owners. In fact, this could cause problems when the parent passes on.

If a gift is made prior to the death of a parent, the basis of the inheritance, is what the parent paid for it. For instance, if the parent paid $100,000 for a home and the child was put on the deed with the parent, when the parent passes away the child's basis for the house is $100,000. This means if they sell the house for $200,000, they will have a gain to pay tax on.

Consider not putting the children on the accounts or deeds. Instead, use a Power of Attorney that allows them authority to manage the property in the event of incapacity.

Then prepare a Will or Trust and designate who will inherit the assets upon the parent's death. This would allow the children to receive the property at a stepped-up basis (fair market value or what it can sell for); which means little or no tax would be paid once the child sells of the inherited property.

Finally, if you put children's names on property and those children go through a divorce or lawsuit, it is possible that your property could also be lost or disposed of because the courts will assume the property is owned jointly by the parent and the child. Not only does putting the children's names on property hurt the children tax-wise, it could hurt the parent both financially and legally, if there is any action taken against the children before the parent passes away.

WEEK #26 – Child and Dependent Care Tax Credits This Summer

Holding those little ones in your arms and slowly guiding them through the path of life, is surely one of the most joyous and fulfilling experience of a lifetime. But there is no denying that it can be hard on your pocketbook. Catherine, a mother of two children aged 7 and 10, experiences this dichotomy between pleasure of child rearing and its pinching effect on the pocketbook. So, to alleviate the effect, you must utilize the option of child and dependent care tax credits to the best of your abilities.

This week we will discuss about child and dependent care tax credits and filing Form 2441. If you have a child under the age of 13, or an incapacitated spouse or parent, you may be able to take a dependent care credit on your individual tax return.

The amount of the credit can be as low as 20 percent (%) of the maximum allowed amount, or as high as 35 percent (%). For 2019 the minimum allowed credit with one child was $600, and the maximum allowed was $1050. With multiple dependents, the minimum allowed credit was $1,200 and the maximum allowed was $2,100. Each year the amount of the credit may change. Your tax professional will know that limit.

To claim this credit, you will need the name, address, and taxpayer identification number of the dependent care provider. The money paid to the provider is income to them that must be reported. You will also need receipts for the payments made to the dependent care provider, to give to your tax preparer. There are certain rules that must be considered to find out if your income level is too high to take this credit, and your tax preparer will be able to help you figure this out.

Some employers offer pre-tax dependent care benefits. If you have dependents that fall into these categories, usually it will be advantageous to use your employer's pre-tax dependent care plan. It will save you taxes to use an employer's plan, but it will also limit the dependent care credit you are eligible for. Your accountant can help with this decision.

Here are 10 facts from the IRS about this important tax credit:

1. You may qualify for the credit if you paid someone to care for your child, dependent or spouse last year.

2. The care you paid for must have been necessary, so you could work or look for work, or attend school. This also applies to your spouse if you are married and filing jointly.

3. The care must have been for 'qualifying persons.' A qualifying person can be your child under age 13. They may also be a spouse or dependent who is physically or mentally incapable of self- care. They must also have lived with you for more than half the year.

4. You, and your spouse if you file jointly, must have earned income, such as wages from a job. Special rules apply to a spouse who is a student or disabled. You can also get a Dependent Care credit up to $500 for each child age 17 and older or a non-child dependent, such as a parent, sibling, aunt, uncle or other extended family member.

5. The payments for care can't go to your spouse, the parent of your qualifying person or to someone you can claim as a dependent on your return. Care payments also can't go to your child under the age of 19, even if the child isn't your dependent.

6. The credit is worth up to 35 percent (%) of the qualifying costs for care, depending on your income. That credit is limited, based on the number of dependents, your childcare expenses and your taxable income.

7. Overnight camp or summer school tutoring costs do not qualify. You can't include the cost of care provided by your spouse or your child who is under age 19 at the end of the year. You also cannot count the cost of care given by a person you can claim as your dependent. Special rules apply if you get dependent care benefits from your employer. For more see Form 2441, Child and Dependent Care Expenses.

8. You must include the Social Security number of each qualifying person to claim the credit. You must report this information when you claim the credit on your tax return.

9. You must include the name, address and identifying number of your care provider to claim the credit. This is usually the Social Security number of an individual or the Employer Identification Number of a business.

10. Remember that this credit is not just a summer tax benefit. You may be able to claim it for care you pay for throughout the year. To claim the credit, attach Form 2441 to your tax return.

Be sure to consider the following, when preparing the Form 2441 for Dependent Care Tax Credits.

Here are some points to remember:

- The maximum amount of expenses allowed for one dependent and multiple dependents is limited each year. Ask Azmoneyguy or your tax professional for the amounts.

- You need the name, address, and taxpayer identification number of the dependent care provider to complete the Form 2441.

- If your employer offers dependent care reimbursement, that will reduce the amount that is available to you, dollar-for-dollar.

- This credit helps reduce regular income tax but may not reduce alternative minimum tax (be sure to see Azmoneyguy or your tax professional for specifics).

WEEK #27 – Teaching Children about Finances and Self Reliance

Doesn't the early bird catch the worm? So, starting early, as early as Kindergarten helps in shaping good financial habits in the long run. When they start identifying, pennies, nickels and dimes in school, it's a good time to help them learn their penny's worth. This week we will discuss about how to teach our children good financial habits. Only a few schools teach children a little about money or finance in their lessons, although if you want your children to pick up good financial habits, you should give them some specific training yourself.

Here are some considerations:

- **Set a good example.**
  Children follow their parents lead and will emulate what they see, so keep your own financial affairs in order.

- **Don't give an allowance.**
  Make children earn money to spend. Allowances encourage expectations of getting something for nothing. Paying for performance says no work or no chores completed means no money given or earned. This way the child can only blame

him or herself for not being paid. (Work means money, extra pay is ok for extra work.)

- **Encourage savings.**

  Children need to learn early that waiting for something pays. The longer they wait, the more money they will have. Teach them the secret of compounding. (Piggy banks are ok - for young children try clear ones so they can watch their money grow, and try savings accounts for older children)

- **Teach money management.**

  Show how to compare interest rates and teach them money doesn't take care of itself.

- **Explain why some money should be saved, some spent, and some given away to charity.**

  Teaching children how to save, spend, and donate teaches children to become better citizens, better taxpayers, and better contributors to society (1/3 saved, 1/3 spent, 1/3 donated is one option)

- **Go to www.kids.gov to learn ways to teach money to kids, teens and adults.**

  This website shows you how to teach money uses and management to children (grades K-5), Teens (grade 6 -8), and grown-ups including teachers and parents. Uses games and videos to both educate and entertain.

Teaching Self Reliance and Financial Confidence

Helping your children financially by teaching self-reliance is one of the greatest gifts you can offer your children. Through teachings and setting a good example, you can help your children become financially responsible and independent adults. However, there is a fine line between helping your kids get started and enabling them to stay dependent. If your children live at home, expect them to contribute to the household. Even full-time students can share household chores and hold down part time jobs to help pay for room and board. If practical, hire your children through your business and expect them to earn those wages.

Before helping your child buy a car, determine whether the purchase is necessary. Are work and/or school within walking distance, is public transportation available, is using a bicycle feasible? If none of these alternatives are viable, enlist your child's aide in finding and buying an affordable, but reliable car. The child should pay at least part of the purchase price and be responsible for insurance and operating costs. Or consider replacing your own vehicle and selling your old car to your child at its trade- in value.

- **Helping your children be self-reliant is a better choice than purchasing something for them**

153

Never give an allowance, instead require certain chores to be performed and pay them for completing. That way, children learn that nothing is free. They also learn if they do not work, they do not get paid.

- **Before purchasing a car for your child, consider replacing your own vehicle**
  Sell your used vehicle to your child at trade-in value. You can find the trade in value online with Kelly Blue Book (**https://www.kbb.com**). This helps the child learn nothing is free. Another technique is to match what the child saves to purchase a car. Again, this teaches the child to work, get paid, and save for the future. Giving a car to a child is not helping them; it's teaching them that someone other than themselves will provide for them.

- **Determine whether the purchase is necessary**
  School/work nearby, public transportation. Children will always want more, no matter how much they have. Teaching them the difference between wants and needs is one of the best lesson's parents can pass on to children. You know what a need is rather than a want; teach this to your children.

- **Make sure the child is paying part of the purchase price and all operating expenses**

Before they get the car or other want, make sure they can afford to keep up the item on a regular basis (gas, oil, tags, insurance, repairs), otherwise you will find yourself paying for the expenses of your kids, rather than teaching them to pay for themselves.

WEEK # 28 – Powers of Attorney (POA)

The knowledge and action to prepare for the future gives you "peace of mind". The present is a gift that we enjoy, but the future is unknown, so to secure yourself and your family for the future, it is necessary to take certain steps in the present. For instance, a lot of people are not aware that a Durable Power of Attorney may be necessary, even if you are married. That way your spouse will be able to act on your behalf, if you are incapacitated.

Nicholas and Martha are aware that unless you have an asset that is joint owned, one doesn't assume the right to speak or act for the other spouse without a Power of Attorney (POA). This POA document may allow others to speak and/or act for you, either in tax, financial, legal or healthcare matters. The person you give permission to act on your behalf is called an Agent. An Agent is the one who represents, and the Principal is the person who needs representation or assistance.

It's important to understand that while the agent has your permission to act, speak, sign, and obligate agreements on your behalf; it is a requirement that the agent put YOUR best interests in front of everyone else, including the agent acting on your behalf. This is known as a fiduciary responsibility. All agents have a fiduciary responsibility to protect the principal they represent in all matters.

If you have a Mental Health or Healthcare (medical) Power of Attorney, be sure to include the Health Insurance Portability and Accountability Act (HIPAA) inclusion paragraph that allows you to receive personal medical information about the principal you represent.

If you act as an agent or POA for anyone, be sure to understand the Agency law of the state you live in. Consult an attorney and have them give you instructions in writing as to your responsibilities as a POA. When signing documents as a POA, always sign your name and the initials "POA" after your signature, to let others know you have permission to act. **Do not sign the name of the principal.** There are many kinds of Powers of Attorney.

Some of the Powers of Attorney are listed below:

- **Immediate Power of Attorney**
  As soon as you sign it, someone can act on your behalf.

- **Springing Power of Attorney**
  It springs into action upon a certain condition (such as incompetence or incapacitation or absence).

- **Durable Power of Attorney**

Husbands and Wives, or partners, should have a Durable Power of Attorney on each other. In some states, if a husband and wife begin to refinance a home and one of them becomes disabled during the finance, a Durable Power of Attorney must be executed prior to the disability, to finish the refinance. (Otherwise a Court Order must be issued naming the spouse or partner as Guardian. This Court Order requires legal fees and an appearance before the court). A Durable Power of Attorney allows financial/legal decisions to be made on your behalf by an agent.

- **Don't forget HIPAA or privacy provisions**
  POA's cannot receive personal info from financial, legal, or healthcare professionals without this addition.

- **Healthcare Power of Attorney**
  Appoints a person (Agent) to make medical decisions for you.

- **Mental Health Power of Attorney**
  Makes mental health decisions for you (check in or out of mental health facility).

- **Living Will**

Directs actions to be taken if condition is terminal or death imminent. This is not a regular Will. It is instructions to discontinue care or "pull the plug", under certain conditions.

WEEK #29 – Control Identity Theft and Credit Scores

Keep impersonators at bay! Along with its boon, the digital era brings with it some trouble as well and identity theft is one problem that is growing and frequency. In the ever-increasing digital space, stealing identity of a person to gain financial advantages has become easier. So, this is one area where people must learn to be more cautious to prevent identity theft.

Mike, a marketing professional working in an advertising agency, is well versed with the fact that there are now a few new weapons to help you battle identity theft. Like Mike, every citizen of this country should be aware that a federal law gives consumers the right to receive a copy of your credit report once every 12 months free of charge, or if you are refused credit on an application. This law was designed to encourage Americans to keep a closer watch on their credit report and reduce identity theft.

Credit Reporting Bureaus

Equifax, TransUnion, and Experian, each are required to provide you with an annual credit file disclosure or report upon request (therefore you must ask for it). Now there are some credit card companies that freely give your credit score on the monthly credit card statements.

On others, you must still request and pay, though, to get a credit score. It is not part of the new free credit report annual provision.

IRS Handling of Identity Theft

The Treasury Inspector General for Tax Administration (TIGTA) reported that the Internal Revenue Service (IRS) failed to investigate thousands of identity theft cases, because taxpayers filed an incorrect tax return. The IRS used Form 3949-A (Information Referral) to report suspected cases of tax fraud in 2012. However, the instructions were very confusing, and many people used this form to report identity theft cases. The IRS destroyed those forms because prior to May 2012, there were no procedures in place to process them as identity theft cases.

Today there are now current IRS procedures in place that allow for Form 3949-A to be accepted as a report for identity theft. If you use this form, you must attach a copy of your police report and valid identification. If you want to report identity theft without sending a copy of your police report and picture identification, the IRS accepts Form 14039 (Identity Theft Affidavit). As soon as you find out your identity has been compromised, you should contact the IRS immediately, along with Credit Reporting Agencies, and your ID theft insurance company; if you have that coverage.

You can report this to the IRS either separately or attached to your tax return. Be sure to also contact everyone you bank with, do business with, and file personal information with, about the ID theft.

Credit bureau reporting is MORE than just reporting credit card usage and history. It includes ALL types of credit activity. Any type of loan, Tax returns, Health insurance and Medicare coverages, Driver's License, Passport and Social Security information all use credit activity to validate your access to them.

How can we protect ourselves from identity theft? Keep these tips from "idexpertscorp.com" in mind:

- File your tax return as early as possible. Fraudsters file early using stolen information in attempts to beat the taxpayer to filing. The IRS easily processes the first return filed under a social security number- make sure it's the legitimate return to avoid delays.

- Any email purporting to be from the IRS is likely a scam. If you have filed online, you will receive emails from the Efile website you used confirming that your return has been accepted by the IRS. You will also receive payment confirmation emails from the IRS if you pay your taxes online directly to the IRS thru their Electronic Federal Tax Payment System (EFTPS).

- **The IRS will never ask for personal or financial information in an email or over the phone.** Never provide your social security number, bank or credit card information, or security- related information such as mother's maiden name in an email or on another site through an email link you were sent.

- Scammers often use bait to get their victims to respond - dangling promises of extra tax refunds or offering payment for participation in an IRS survey. Another tactic involves the use of threats of legal action or withholding of refunds. Remember, the IRS will not communicate with consumers for any of these purposes via email.

- Be cautious when visiting the IRS website. Always go to https://www.irs.gov directly rather than following any email links to the site. There are many false websites impersonating the IRS, waiting for unsuspecting consumers to enter their personal information. Common scams often try to direct consumers via email to phony IRS sites. Remember that an email link's true website address (URL) is revealed by moving your mouse over the link.
- If you leave your taxes to the professionals, it pays to be choosy when choosing a tax preparer. Unethical tax preparers are making headlines every day for committing tax fraud or identity theft using their clients' information. It's important to check your preparer's credentials or licensing. Be sure to only

use a Certified Public Accountant (CPA), Enrolled Agent (EA), or attorney.

- You may also use either a Credit Freeze or a Fraud Alert on your credit account at the reporting agencies to stop the further use of your information to acquire financial access of your accounts. Each Credit Reporting agency will charge a monthly fee for a Credit Freeze, while a Fraud Alert is usually free, for all three. And a Fraud Alert is only necessary to send to one credit agency, (www.experian.com/fraud) because the other two will be notified. Either method will slow down your use of credit, going forward because you will need to approve or verify your identity before your credit purchase will be accepted. SO, remember, this will slow your use of credit!

Income Tax and Social Security Impact of Identity Theft

Remember this, reporting Identity Theft to the IRS will delay your refund, but it will also ensure that you receive it rather than the ID thief. Chances are you will receive a check, rather than direct deposit refund into your checking or savings account. Also, you will receive an ID Theft personal identification number (PIN) to use when filing future returns to ensure your return is the correct one.

If you end up spending money to prosecute an identity thief, either through attorney's fees or other fines, the out of pocket money may be considered a Casualty Loss. This could be an allowed deduction on your personal tax return.

Casualty losses are given a better tax deduction than a normal itemized deduction. It is considered an Ordinary Loss, is not subject to Alternative Minimum Taxes, and could help you reduce your tax liability against any other income you might have.

Further, if you are a victim of identity theft, you must paper file your tax return. You cannot e- file your return! Be sure to attach a completed and signed IRS Form 14039, along with a copy of your current driver's license or passport, to be submitted with your original tax return. This will ensure your refund is sent to you and your tax records are correctly placed in your name. This is also important to make sure your Social Security records reflect correct information towards your benefits later in life.

Here are several steps the IRS suggests you can take to help protect yourself against identity theft:

- Don't give a business your SSN or ITIN just because they ask. Give it only when required.

- Protect your financial information.

- Check your credit report at least every 12 months.

- Check your Social Security statement or account at least every 12 months.

- Protect your personal computers by using firewalls and anti-spam/virus software, updating security patches and changing passwords for Internet accounts regularly.

- Don't give personal information over the phone, through the mail or on the Internet unless you have initiated the contact and are sure of the recipient.

Here are some final points to remember:

- **All three credit reporting bureaus are required to give an annual credit report (if requested). But you must still pay to acquire a credit score from the credit reporting companies**

- **Ways to get credit reports are as follows:**

  ✓ **Visit the website at www.annualcreditreport.com**

✓ Write to:

Annual Credit Report Request Service

P.O. BOX 105283

Atlanta, GA 30348

✓ Call: Toll Free at (877) 322-8228

- Use **IRS** form **14039** along with a copy of your driver's license or passport to file with your original tax return. If you are a victim of identity theft, this will ensure your refund is sent to you, and you will be sure your income records are corrected with the Social Security Administration.

- Contact your bank, credit card companies, Social Security Administration and all financial institutions you are associated with.

- Consider using either a Fraud Alert or Credit Freeze on your credit report, if you have been exposed to hacking, theft or loss. Freezes cost a monthly fee, while Fraud Alerts are free.

- **Contact your tax professional to seek assistance on instructions.**

WEEK #30 - Keeping Records Safe — Tax and others

In life, you never know what is waiting for you in the next turn ahead. Threats like hurricanes, tornadoes, floods, fires or some other natural disasters, break-ins, vandalism, electronic hacking and other malicious events might be prowling around waiting to pounce on you anytime during the year. You never know when a disaster will strike, or what damage it will cause. There may be little or nothing you can do to prevent your home or office from being destroyed or damaged, but you can at least ensure that no matter what happens, your tax, financial and other personal records will be safe.

Oliver, a doctor by profession, understood the importance of safe upkeep and maintenance of personal and financial records, especially to cope during unforeseen circumstances. Everyone should have a plan in place for disaster recovery of records to prove ownership or relationship. These are records that insurance companies and federal, state and local governments require to assist you in recovery of loss.

Your insurance company will need proof of what you lost to replace your items. The government will need proof of ownership of real estate, cars, personal items and birth certificates to prove who your dependents are and to assist you in providing low cost or no interest loans. Some government programs as the Federal Emergency

Management Agency (FEMA) even give you free money after a disaster, depending on what records you provide to prove what you owned and who your family is.

You can take a few simple steps to protect your tax and financial records in case of a disaster:

- **Backup records electronically**

  Keep an extra set of electronic records in a safe place, away from where you store the originals. You can use cloud storage, a flash drive, an external hard drive, CD or DVD to store the most important records. You can take these with you to keep your copies safe. You may want to store items such as bank statements, tax returns and insurance policies.

- **Document valuables**

  Take pictures or videotape the contents of your home or place of business. These may help you prove the value of your lost items for insurance claims and casualty loss deductions.

- **Update emergency plans**

  Review your emergency plans every year. You may need to update them if your family personal or business situation changes.

- **Obtain a security plan checklist**

  IRS publication 4557, "Safeguarding Taxpayer Data", is a great place to start. It can help you take additional steps to protect your personal, financial, and tax data.

- **Keep a GO BAG handy**

  A GO BAG is a suitcase, duffle bag, pillowcase or anything to hold emergency items to take with you in the event of an emergency evacuation. Things like money, checkbook, credit cards, medications, jewelry, coins, something to communicate with, or light a fire with, eye protection, solar chargers, clothes for at least 5 days, water, food, just to name a few items and anything you feel you can carry around with you to use until help arrives. Be sure to keep your family jewels with you!

How to obtain copies of lost or destroyed tax returns?

We can provide you with a copy of your lost or destroyed tax returns, if we prepared the returns, at no cost for current clients (see online portal below), or for non-current clients we charge a small fee and you do not have to wait for a copy to be mailed to you from the IRS. If you can't find your copies, the IRS can give you a transcript of the information you need, or a copy of your tax return. Remember though, a transcript is NOT a copy of your return, just a printout of your return information. **They are NOT the same thing.**

Here's how to get your federal tax return information from the IRS:

- Transcripts are free and you can get them for the current year and the past three years. In most cases, a transcript includes the tax information you need.

- A tax return transcript shows most line items from the tax return that you filed. It also includes items from any accompanying forms and schedules that you filed. It doesn't reflect any change that you or the IRS made, after you filed your original return.

- A tax account transcript includes your marital status, the type of return you filed, your adjusted gross income and taxable income. It does include any changes that you or the IRS made to your tax return after you filed it.

- You can get your free transcripts by phone, by mail or by fax within five to 10 days from the time IRS receives your request.

✓ To order by phone, call 800-908-9946 and follow the prompts. You can also request your transcript using your smartphone with the **IRS2Go** mobile phone app.

✓ To request an individual tax return transcript by mail or fax, complete **Form 4506T-EZ**, Short Form Request for Individual Tax Return Transcript. Businesses and individuals who need a tax account transcript should use **Form 4506-T**, Request for Transcript of Tax Return.

• If you need a copy of your filed and processed tax return, the IRS will charge a fee for each tax year. You should complete **Form 4506**, Request for Copy of Tax Return, to make the request. Mail it to the IRS address listed on the form for your area. Copies are generally available for the current year and past six years. You should allow 75 days for delivery. If your state has an income tax, contact the Department of Revenue or Franchise Tax Board to obtain copies of current and past years' state tax returns as well, for a fee.

The IRS has a Disaster Hotline to help people with tax issues after a disaster. Call the IRS at 1- 866-562-5227 to speak with a specialist trained to handle disaster-related tax issues. There is no fee to request records for disaster survivors.

Don't forget about an online portal. Remember, our current clients have access to copies of tax returns at no cost when you visit our website at **www.azmoneyguy.com**. If you need your login information or tips on how to use the portal to your advantage, let us know.

WEEK #31 -Tax Benefits of Adoption

When you take care of someone, you are also taken care of! It's like Karma. You do good, you get back good in return. Ben and Stephanie had adopted a baby girl because they felt their family wasn't complete otherwise. This act of adopting children is not only a good and kind deed where another human being is benefiting from your benevolence, but in doing so you get assistance from Uncle Sam.

This week we will discuss some of the tax benefits of taking advantage of the adoption credit opportunity. This tax credit is taken in the year the child is awarded to you by the courts, as your adopted child and the adoption is final. Sometimes, you may pay for the adoption money early, last year for example, but when you finalize the adoption is when you get the tax credit.

Here are some points to consider for expenses used as an adoption credit:

- **All expenses used to adopt a child, are given as a tax credit for up to the limit on IRS Tables**
  Adoptions prior to 2012 receive a refundable tax credit. Today, the tax credit is non-refundable. This means you will not get a check from the IRS for adoption, just reduce your

taxes down to zero. Refundable credits may give you a check for the credit amount. This is one tax benefit that does NOT require you to keep receipts for the adoption expenses. Be sure to ask us about whether you need to keep receipts or not for this benefit.

- **Each dollar of tax credit may be equivalent up to $3 of tax deduction**
  This is because a tax credit reduces your tax directly, while a tax deduction only reduces the income which is taxed, but the true benefit depends on your tax bracket.

- **The credit starts to phase out when your household income exceeds certain IRS limits**
  The IRS publishes annually of the income phase out for this limit. Ask us what the phase out limit is for this year.

- **Employers can also pay for adoption expenses and receive a tax credit of the same amount as individuals**
  Self-employed individuals may claim a tax credit through their C-Corporation, but owners of S-Corporations claim the credit on their personal returns.

- **For 2020 and later you can distribute (Penalty Free) up to $10,000 per parent from retirement accounts**

  This is part of the new SECURE Act, that allows parents to take money out of retirement accounts in order to help pay to adopt a child.

- **Special needs children qualify for even bigger tax credits**

  Be sure you understand the "special needs" description. It is wider in scope than you think. For instance, abused (defined more than just sexually for this tax benefit) children may qualify as special needs.

WEEK #32 - Uninsured and Underinsured Motorists Insurance Coverage and Umbrella Insurance

Your safety is in your own hands. So, when out on the road, it is your duty to ensure your safety. Danny, a first-time car-buyer was conscious of his role in fortifying his own safety while out on the road. Many states have a minimum law that requires motorists prove financial responsibility when driving on the road. You either must purchase the minimum auto insurance or you must post a bond.

For example, as of 2019, the minimum Arizona insurance coverage provisions are: $15,000 bodily injury per person, $30,000 bodily injury per accident, and $10,000 property damage.

For 2020, Arizona minimum limits increased to $25,000 bodily injury per person, $50,000 bodily injury per accident, and $15,000 property damage.

The National Safety Council tells us:

- The average vehicle on the road costs about $30,000 and the average hospital stay, because of an auto accident, runs about $60,000. This explains that the minimum insurance is not usually enough. So, be sure you purchase greater limits than just mentioned.

- Additionally, in Arizona, 11% of all vehicles on the road do not have **ANY** auto insurance coverage.
There is a coverage known as Uninsured and Underinsured Motorist for Bodily Injury (UMBI). This insurance protects you if you are hit by someone with little or no insurance. Arizona does **NOT** offer uninsured and underinsured property damage. Your property damage (collision/comprehensive insurance) will take over if the person who hits you, does not have enough property coverage. This explains the need to make sure that your coverage is higher than the minimum. So, check with your state to see if you can buy Uninsured or Underinsured Property Damage (UMPD).

The uninsured and underinsured motorist coverage will protect you for medical purposes, if somebody hits you, sending you to the hospital or doctor. If you don't purchase this type of coverage, **YOUR** insurance policy will have to pay your medical bills. If your insurance must pay your medical expenses, you might experience increased premiums, even if it wasn't your fault. This is another reason to purchase the uninsured and underinsured coverage. The same problem can occur if your state allows purchase of (UMPD) and you choose not to buy it.

Another insurance policy to consider is Umbrella Insurance. Here, the umbrella policy will kick in, if your other insurance is not enough to cover the costs, coverages, medical and property damage that you are involved in. You might think of just buying minimum coverage, then buy high umbrella, but remember, insurance companies are on to this.

Insurance companies usually require that you buy higher insurance coverage before allowing you to buy umbrella policies. Umbrella Insurance Coverage is good for both accidents on the road or at home. If friends or family are injured or hurt at your home, office, or while in your vehicle, and you don't have enough insurance to cover the damages, your Umbrella policy may protect you from filing bankruptcy or suffering major financial distress, from potential law suits even from family and friends that are hurt while on your property. Check with your insurance provider about Umbrella Insurance Coverage.

Here are some points to remember:

- **Minimum Arizona insurance is not enough to cover most accidents**

- **Minimum Arizona insurance limits increased in 2020**

- **Underinsured and uninsured motorist is for bodily injury only in Arizona, but other states offer property damage coverage, in addition.**

- **Not buying this additional insurance could easily increase your premiums, even though the accident is not your fault**

- **Always consider umbrella insurance as another form of protection from potential lawsuits**

WEEK #33 – Higher Education Costs Can Reduce Taxes

It's 'Back to School' time and every one of you must be busy preparing for the academic year ahead. Along with students, even parents are busy gearing up for the new school year. Education is a holistic process, where the students are the ones who focus on studying, but you parents are also equally involved in ensuring that your students are getting access to the best of resources throughout their school years. Trina and Paul are parents to teenagers, who are all set to fly out of their nest. So, while the parents are psychologically preparing themselves to beat the empty nest syndrome, they are also actively looking out for options that can be availed to benefit them financially, at a time when big expenses like tuition fees are awaiting them.

Since school is back in session, so let's discuss some school tax benefits while it's fresh in peoples' minds.

Tuition Expenses

Tuition expenses are available up to $4000. Tuition credits are limited, based on adjusted gross income. Parents can take this deduction if paying for education expenses for themselves, or their children and other dependents, if they claim the child or dependent on the tax return. Be sure to only claim what you pay for, what the 1098-T (this is the form the school sends every January for the past year) says the tuition amount is. The form 1098-T comes to the address of the student, even though the parents might pay the tuition. Be sure you keep the form 1098-T when preparing your tax returns, in order to prove the amount paid for tuition, along with your receipts of payments made. Grants and scholarships that pay for tuition are not payments you can take on your return, but they do reduce the costs of school. You can only claim what you pay for. Be sure to include books, fees, and supplies you pay for as well in the education expenses. Depending on your income and circumstances, you might be able to get a deduction without itemizing or take a tax credit; whichever is better.

The American Opportunity Credit is:

- Worth up to $2,500 per eligible student.

- Only available for the first four years at an eligible college or vocational school.

- Subtracted from your taxes but can also give you a refund of up to $1,000 if it's more than your taxes.

- For students earning a degree or other recognized credential.

- For students going to school at least half-time for at least one academic period that started during the tax year.

- For the cost of tuition, books and required fees and supplies.

The Lifetime Learning Credit is:

- Limited to $2,000 per tax return, per year, no matter how many students qualify.

- For all years of higher education, including classes for learning or improving job skills.

- Limited to the amount of your taxes.

- For the cost of tuition and required fees, plus books, supplies and equipment you must buy from the school.

<u>For both credits:</u>

- Your school should give you a Form 1098-T, Tuition Statement, showing expenses for the year. Make sure it's correct.

- You must file Form 8863, Education Credits, to claim these credits on your tax return.

- You can't claim either credit if someone else claims you as a dependent.

- You can't claim both credits for the same student or for the same expense, in the same year.

- The credits are subject to income limits that could reduce the amount you can claim on your return.

- Employers can deduct up to $5250 (for 2018) as Post-Secondary Education Degree Program Expenses, per employee, through the business, without the employee paying taxes on the money. (This benefit can save taxes for both the employee and the employer.)

- Consider hiring your family and then certain college expenses can be a deduction in the business, if the class is necessary for the employee's job (See the point listed above and consider where it's better to hire your kids through your existing business as employees. Then the college courses or programs might be a complete deduction through your business as an expense. It's possible to even get a tax deduction through the business for college expenses AND can get an education credit for the same expenses; either for the parent and/or the child. Be sure to see your tax preparer to find out the specifics for your circumstances.)

- Employers can also deduct College Education classes paid for employees. The Employer's company may pay for the college classes for employees if there is no discrimination among employees and if the classes will improve the existing job skills of the employees taking the class. If the class is not relevant to the existing job description of the employee, then the previously mentioned limit of $5,250 applies as an employee fringe benefit.

WEEK #34 - Save Taxes with 529 Education Plans

In the list of 'to do' items after childbirth and child rearing, parents often include the 529 Education plans as well. You want to secure your child's future by investing in this piggy bank for the education of your children. Megan and Derrick, first time parents, did not want to waste much time, so they invested in 529 Education plan within a month of their child's birth.

The 529 Education plans have been around since 1996. It is named after Internal Revenue Code (IRC) section 529 and is officially known as a "Qualified Tuition Program". This is an education vehicle that provides for money to be set aside and/or invested and later used for someone (usually a child) to be able to attend school, and have the education paid for.

The BIG benefit is that the earnings or income is NOT subject to tax, if the money taken from the 529 plan is used for education purposes. Each state can offer either a Prepaid Tuition Plan or a Savings Plan. Moreover, you do not need to buy a plan in the state you live in. For instance, you can choose to buy a 529 Savings Plan in Utah, while you are living in Arizona.

But, beware, if you buy the 529 Prepaid Tuition Plan, because in that case you must go to the state's schools! Also, with Prepaid Tuition plans you usually don't even earn as much in the 529 Prepaid Tuition Plan, as you do with the 529 Savings Plan.

You can own the 529 plan, but set it up for your children, grand-children or relatives, friends or even yourself. There is an Owner or Custodian and one beneficiary, per plan. The beneficiary can be changed without any problem, too. So, if your child, that was designated to benefit from the 529 plan, decides not to go to college, you can designate someone else (anyone). You can even roll money from one 529 plan into a 529 plan of another person, without restrictions. There are no limits on who can set up 529 plans, nor is there a limit on how many 529 plans you can own.

How does it work?
You set up a 529 plan and fund it with money.

How much?
There are certain limits, (be sure to see your tax professional) but let's say for now, at least $250 and up to $110,000 in one year. Whatever that account earns while it sits there, is tax deferred AND completely tax free when the money is used for eligible education purposes. So, remember, it's easy to set up a 529 plan, anyone can do it, and make sure you have enough TIME to keep it invested, before you use any

of it, for education. As with all investing, the more time you must wait, the more you usually gain from the investments.

The types of Educational Institutions that qualify to be used with 529 plans are:

Any school, public, private, or faith-based (1st grade through 12th grade)

OR

Any college, university, apprenticeship, vocational, trade school, or primary, secondary and post-secondary institution that can participate in a student aid program administered by the Department of Education.

To get tax free treatment of 529 withdrawals, you must spend the money on Eligible Education Purposes. Examples of this are: tuition, resource fees, books, supplies, registration fees, computers, technology, hardware, software or related equipment, even internet services, room and board. Primary and secondary schools have annual limits on both the amount spent ($10,000 for 2019), while there are no limits placed on expenses paid post-secondary education institutions. **For 2020, you can now use 529 withdrawals to repay student loans and interest, up to $10,000 as well.**

Another possible benefit for 529 plans is that many states offer tax deductions for contributions made to 529 plans, like Arizona offers a $4000 (married couple-2018) deduction, while Colorado offers up to $100,000 (for 2018) as a state tax deduction for that much contributed to a 529 plan!

Be sure to check with Azmoneyguy or another tax professional for current limits.

Look out for "the catch"

As with most tax deferred programs there is a catch. For instance, if you take money out of a 529 plan that is NOT used for education, there is a tax on the earnings amount withdrawn AND a 10% penalty. So be sure to see your tax professional before taking any withdrawals.

Here are some points to remember:

- 529 plans are either Prepaid Tuition plans or Savings plans

- Anyone can set up a 529 plan for anyone, including yourself

- 529 plans are available for primary, secondary, religious, post-secondary, apprenticeship, vocational and trade school educational institutions

- 529 withdrawals can now be used to repay student loans

- The longer you wait to withdraw funds, the more opportunity to grow the plan

- Earnings are tax deferred AND tax free, if used for Eligible Education Purposes

- Eligible Education Purposes include almost everything, but amounts are limited for primary and secondary schools

- Check with your state to see if there are deductions for 529 contributions

- Watch out for tax AND 10% penalty, if non-qualified withdrawals are taken

Robert F Hockensmith

WEEK #35 –Tax Credits That Can Reduce Your Taxes

Credit often causes smiles. Be it a good credit history or taking credit for doing something good, the word 'credit' usually has a positive connotation to it. This is especially true with tax credits. They help you reduce the taxes you owe. A tax credit is almost always better than a tax deduction because it reduces your taxes, dollar for dollar (i.e. - $5 in tax credits reduce your taxes by $5), while tax deductions only reduce your income and then you compute the tax owed from the reduced income (i.e. - $5 in tax deductions only reduce your taxes by $1 if you are in the 20% tax bracket). Dylan and Margaret were aware of this, so they wanted to optimally capitalize on this.

Some credits are also refundable. That means even if you owe no tax, you may still get a refund check. And some are non-refundable, which only reduces your income tax down to zero. The Adoption Tax Credit is one that is non-refundable. You can get approximately $14,080 (2019) in tax credits, but it will not give you a refund if your taxes are less than the credit. So, it's better to receive a refundable credit, but ANY credit is good and almost always better than tax deductions.

Here are some other tax credits you shouldn't overlook when filing your federal tax return:

1. **The Earned Income Tax Credit (EITC)**

   This is a refundable credit for people who work, but don't report earning much money. It can boost your refund by as much as $6,557 (2019 amounts). You may be eligible for the credit based on the amount of your income, your filing status and the number of children in your family. Single workers with no dependents may also qualify for EITC. Remember, if you are audited and it is determined that you are not eligible for the Earned Income Credit that you claimed, you could be barred from applying for Earned Income Credit for ten (10) years. This penalty comes because some people tried to apply for the tax credit, but the returns were fraudulent.

   Now tax preparers must ask more questions and see some proof from taxpayers, such as birth certificates, medical records, social security cards, school records, divorce decree or some other form of proof that the dependent is living with you, and you are able to take the dependent on your tax return. Visit IRS.gov and use the **EITC Assistant tool** to see if you can claim this credit. For more see **Publication 596,** Earned Income Credit.

2. **The Child Tax Credit (CTC) and Dependent Care Credit (DCC)**

   This can help you offset the cost of daycare or day camp for children under age 13. You may also be able to claim it for costs paid to care for a disabled spouse or non-child dependent of any age. For details, see **Publication 503**, Child and Dependent Care Expenses. This type of credit can reduce the taxes you pay by as much as $2,000 for each qualified child you claim on your tax return. The child must be under age 17 in 2019 and meets other requirements. Use the **Interactive Tax Assistant tool** on IRS.gov to see if you can claim the credit. **See Publication 972**, Child Tax Credit, for more about the rules. If you care for a parent, sibling or other non-child dependent, or you have dependent children, age 17 or older, who are not disabled you may qualify for a $500 Dependent Care credit, depending on income limits. Disabled children or other dependents usually qualify for CTC and/or DCC at any age, subject to income limits.

3. **The Retirement Savings Credit**

This helps workers save for retirement. You may qualify if your income is $64,000 or less in 2019 and you contribute to an IRA or a retirement plan at work. Check out **Publication 590**, Individual Retirement Arrangements (IRAs).

Did you, your spouse or your dependent take higher education classes last or this year?

If so, you may be able to claim some education credits such as the American Opportunity Credit or the Lifetime Learning Credit to help cover the costs.

4. The American Opportunity Credit is:

- Worth up to $2,500 per eligible student.

- Only available for the first four years at an eligible college or vocational school.

- Subtracted from your taxes but can also give you a refund of up to $1,000, if it's more than your taxes.

- For students earning a degree or other recognized credential.

- For students going to school at least half-time or at least one academic period that started during the tax year.

- For the cost of tuition, books and required fees and supplies.

5. The Lifetime Learning Credit is:

- Limited to $2,000 per tax return, per year, no matter how many students qualify.

- For all years of higher education, including classes for learning or improving job skills.

- Limited to the amount of your taxes.

- For the cost of tuition and required fees, plus books, supplies and equipment you must buy from the school.

For both School credits:

- Your school should give you a Form 1098-T, Tuition Statement, showing tuition paid for the year. Make sure it's correct.

- You must file **Form 8863**, Education Credits, to claim these credits on your tax return.

- You can claim **only one type of education credit per student** on your federal tax return each year. If more than one student qualifies for a credit in the same year, you can claim a different credit for each student. For example, you can claim the AOTC for one student and claim the LLC for the other student.

Eligible schools are those that offer education beyond high school. This includes most colleges and universities. Vocational schools or other postsecondary schools may also qualify.

- You can't claim either credit if someone else claims you as a dependent.

- You can't claim both credits for the same student or for the same expense, in the same year.

- The credits are subject to income limits that could reduce the amount you can claim on your return.

Nonresident alien. If you are in the U.S. on an F-1 student visa, you usually file your federal tax return as a nonresident alien. You can't claim an education credit if you were a nonresident alien for any part of the tax year unless you elect to be treated as a resident alien for federal tax purposes. To learn more about these rules, see **Publication 519**, U.S. Tax Guide for Aliens.

Income limits. These credits are subject to income limitations and may be reduced or eliminated, based on your income.

6. **Foreign Tax Credits and Exclusions**

Some taxpayers earn interest and dividend income from foreign investments. Some of the income comes from investing in mutual funds or exchange traded funds (ETF). That income sometimes require that the taxpayer pays foreign taxes, to the government, where the investments are located. Some taxpayers work outside of the United States and must pay foreign income taxes on the income they earn overseas. If US taxpayers pay foreign taxes, either from wages or investments, the amount of the foreign taxes paid, is considered a credit against US tax, on their personal tax return. This may be accomplished by completing IRS Form 1116. (irs.gov/forms), or taking the deduction on Schedule A, under TAXES section. Your tax preparer would be able to determine which of the two options is best for you, based on your circumstances.

Also, when Americans work overseas for foreign companies, there is an exclusion allowed each year by the IRS (azmoneyguy would know how much is allowed for this year).

This exclusion or credit is non-refundable. A non-refundable credit means the amount of the credit can reduce or eliminate Federal Income taxes, but any excess credit will not be given back to the taxpayer, as a refund. You can't get refunds from this credit, only tax reduction, but the exclusion, deduction or credit can reduce your income taxes to ZERO.

- **US taxpayers may be able to get a tax credit for paying taxes in a different country for earning income from interest, or dividends**
- **You have a choice of claiming the taxes on Schedule A or Form 1116, whichever benefits you most**
- **The tax benefit is a non-refundable credit. This means you can reduce or eliminate tax down to ZERO**
- **Some income earned from a foreign company in a foreign country by Americans, can be excluded each year from paying taxes on it. See your tax professional for each year's excluded amount**

And finally, here are some energy credits to consider:

7. **Non-Business Energy Property Credit (available thru 2020)**

- This credit is worth 10 percent of the cost of certain qualified energy-saving items you added to your main home last year. This includes items such as insulation, windows, doors and roofs, heat pumps, water heaters, air conditioners, furnaces, air circulating fans are but a few examples of items that qualify for the credit.

- You may also be able to claim the credit for the actual cost and installation of certain property. This may include items such as water heaters and heating and air conditioning systems named above. Each type of property has a different dollar limit.

- This credit has a maximum lifetime limit of $500. You may only use $200 of this limit for windows.

- Your main home must be in the U.S. to qualify for the credit.

- Be sure you have the written certification from the manufacturer that their product qualifies for this tax credit. They usually post it on their website or include it with the product's packaging. You can rely on it to claim the credit, but do not attach it to your return. Keep it with your tax records.

8. **Residential Energy Efficient Property Credit**

- This tax credit is 30 percent of the cost of alternative energy equipment installed on or in your home.

- Qualified equipment includes solar hot water heaters, solar electric equipment and wind turbines, geothermal heaters and pumps.

- There is no dollar limit on the credit for most types of property. If your credit is more than the tax you owe, you can carry forward the unused portion of this credit to next year's tax return.

- The home must be in the U.S. It does not have to be your main home.

- This credit is available in 2019.

- Use **Form 5695**, Residential Energy Credits, to claim these Energy credits.

    Also, always check with your state to see if it offers energy tax credits or deductions too!

Robert F Hockensmith

WEEK #36 — Ten Tax Facts if You Sell Your Home and Reverse Mortgages

Do you know that if you sell your home and make a profit, the gain may not be taxable? Anna and Jenny have recently learned about this from their tax professional so now they are deliberating over the idea of selling their 15-years-old home. The fact that the profit, you make from selling your old home, is not taxable is just one key tax rule that you should know.

Here are ten facts to keep in mind if you sell your home this year:

1. If you have a capital gain on the sale of your home, you may be able to exclude your gain from tax. This rule may apply if you owned and used it as your main home for at least two (2) out of the five (5) years before the date of sale. And if you moved out and started renting your residence, you may have complicated rules to follow when you sell. Be sure to seek professional advice, these special rules can be complex.

2. There are exceptions to the ownership and use rules. Some exceptions apply to persons with a disability. Some apply to certain members of the military and certain government and

207

Peace Corps workers. For details see **Publication 523**, Selling Your Home.

3. The most gain you can exclude is $250,000. This limit is $500,000 for joint returns. The **Net Investment Income Tax** will not apply to the excluded gain.

4. If the gain is not taxable, you still need to report the sale to the IRS on your tax return, even if there is no tax owed on the sale.

5. You must also report the sale on your tax return if you can't exclude all or part of the gain. And you must report the sale if you choose not to claim the exclusion. That's also true if you get Form 1099-S, Proceeds from Real Estate Transactions. If you report the sale you should review the **Questions and Answers on the Net Investment Income Tax** on IRS.gov.

6. Generally, you can exclude the gain from the sale of your main home only once every two years.

7. If you own more than one home, you may only exclude the gain on the sale of your main home. Your main home usually

is the home that you live in most of the time. You can only have one principal residence at a time.

8. If you claimed the first-time homebuyer credit when you bought the home, special rules apply to the sale. For more on those rules see **Publication 523**.

9. If you sell your main home (residence) at a loss, you can't deduct it.

10. After you sell your home and move, be sure to give your new address to your tax preparer and the IRS. You can send the IRS a completed **Form 8822**, Change of Address, to do this.

Reverse Mortgages

Reverse Mortgages are becoming more popular with the aging population. A reverse mortgage is a way for senior citizens to take advantage of the equity in their home and still live somewhat comfortably. It's the opposite of a traditional mortgage.

With a traditional mortgage, you borrow money to purchase a home and then pay off the debt. With a reverse mortgage, you receive loan proceeds as a lump-sum payout, an annuity, a line of credit, or a combination of the three. But you make no mortgage payments if you reside in the property, but you are still responsible for annual property taxes and homeowner's insurance. The loan with any accrued interest comes due when you move out or pass away.

To qualify for reverse mortgages, you must be at least 62 years old and own the home outright (or have a balance that can be paid off with the loan proceeds). How much you can borrow depends on your age, the home's market value, and interest rates.

As always, there is a downside to reverse mortgages. Closing costs can be very steep, as much as 5% of the home's value. In addition, borrowers may have to purchase mortgage insurance and they are still on the hook for property taxes and homeowner's insurance each year.

Federal Truth in Lending Laws requires lenders to provide information about interest rates, payment terms, and other costs in writing to anyone who agrees to or enquires about a reverse mortgage.

The Federal government also requires interested homeowners to take a class conducted by Housing and Urban Development (HUD) to learn all the rules of reverse mortgages. Your mortgage lender can give you more information on the class. The class is free and can be taken online as well. You receive a Certificate of Completion that goes to the lender to prove you have attended the class.

If you are interested, shop for a reverse mortgage just as you would for any other loan. Make sure the basic terms of competing loans are comparable, and then go with the lowest price by comparing interest rates, upfront fees, and other charges.

Where many seniors get in trouble, with reverse mortgages, is that they forget that they are individually responsible for annual homeowner's insurance and real estate taxes! When the mortgage company is paying it with your mortgage payments, there is nothing to worry if they are paid, but when you take a reverse mortgage, YOU are required to pay your insurance and taxes separately. **The mortgage company will not do it for you!**

Mortgage interest is only deductible if you are paying it with reverse mortgage. Unless you pay the interest, there is no deduction for interest accumulated.

Here are some bullets to remember:

- Usually selling personal residence is tax free

- Exemption amount varies with marital status, work conditions and medical status

- Military and Government workers have preferential rules for gain exemption

- Gain exempted can be up to $500,000 for married and $250,000 for single taxpayers, as often as every two years

- Reverse mortgages are a way to live on a home's equity

- Must be at least 62 years old and own the home to qualify

- You must take a one-day class before getting a reverse mortgage

- No payments made until you move out or pass away

- Costs can be steep (upfront fees 5%, mortgage insurance premiums, interest rates) and you are still responsible for property taxes and insurance

- Shop reverse mortgages like other loans

- Remember that the homeowner is responsible for paying the insurance and property taxes themselves (The mortgage company does not pay it, for you.)

- Mortgage interest isn't deductible unless you are paying it. **Accumulating interest is not deductible.**

WEEK #37 – Children Employed by Parents who own a business

While rolling out a roadmap for their future professional growth, employing children in your own business also works to your advantage from the tax perspective. As a self-employed business owner (sole proprietorship), paying wages to a child can be an effective way to shift income from the taxpayer who owns the business to the child, who usually is in a lower income bracket.

Jamie, proprietor of a small bed and breakfast, and a mother, employed her daughter, Devin, in her business. This way she could not only help her daughter understand her finances well and make her literally work for it, but this move also helped both mother and daughter in saving taxes.

It may even be possible to escape taxes completely on wages paid to the child. The child can contribute to a retirement plan and may be able to take a tax credit for education expenses. Make sure the employed child serves a genuine purpose working for the parent.

The child could perform an administrative or small function in the parent's business. This way the wages paid would be a legitimate expense of the business. You need to make sure that you do not violate any child labor or minimum wage laws. Always be sure to keep track of your children's time while working for you. The presence of a completed timecard or time record is the BEST way to help prove when and how long your child worked for you or your company.

When the employer is in a sole proprietorship and the child is under the age of 18, there is no social security tax to be withheld. Each year the amount the child can earn without paying ANY taxes varies. And any wages paid by the parent-owner of a sole proprietorship to the child, is a business expense for the owner. Be sure to see your tax professional, if you own your own business and have children, to discuss the benefits of paying wages to your children.

Paying children allows the business to pay fringe benefits for the child through the business as well. Benefits covered could be health insurance, college education, retirement contributions, business trips and more. Your tax professional knows these rules, limitations and the many benefits there are to hire your children.

Here are some of the benefits of parents employing children:

- **No FICA Tax on child's wages up to 18 years old** (Saves thousands of dollars annually for parents who pay children)

- **No Federal Income Tax on child's wages up to the standard deduction** (Again, this can save both parents and children from paying hundreds or thousands in taxes, per child, each year)

- **Ability to contribute to child's retirement** (Children who get paid can contribute into an IRA each year)

- **Ability to claim travel and employee benefit expenses for the child from the business**

- **Ability to pay for health expenses and insurance through the company**

- **Stay within all child labor and minimum wage laws** (Check with Azmoneyguy or your tax professional for the rules)

- Always keep a completed timecard or record of when and how long the child worked for you or your company, and a description of their duties performed.

WEEK #38 - IRS Online Tools for Year-Round Tax Help

Help is just a click away. Getting year-round tax help from the IRS is easier than ever before. The IRS website has many online tools that you can use to get the service you need. Greg, an engineer by profession knows this, so he never shies away from visiting the IRS website for his tax-related queries. For example, with IRS.gov you can e-file your tax return for free, easily check the status of your refund, or get many of your tax questions answered.

Here are some of the online tools that the IRS offers to make filing your taxes less taxing:

- **IRS Free File.**
  You can use **IRS Free File** to prepare and e-file your federal tax return for free. Free File will do much of the work for you with brand-name tax software or Fillable Forms. If you still need to file your 2018 tax return, Free File is available through Oct. 15, annually. The only way to use IRS Free File is through the IRS website.

- **Where's My Refund?**

  Checking the status of your tax refund is easy when you use **Where's My Refund?** You can also use this tool with the **IRS2Go mobile app**.

- **Direct Pay.**

  Use our **Direct Pay** service to pay your tax bill or pay your estimated tax directly from your checking or savings account. Direct Pay is safe, easy and free. The tool walks you through five simple steps to pay your tax in one online session.

- **Online Payment Agreement.**

  If you can't pay your taxes in full, apply for an **Online Payment Agreement** at https://www.irs.gov. The Direct Debit payment plan option is a lowest-cost hassle-free way to make monthly payments.

- **Withholding Calculator.**

  If you got a larger refund or owed more tax than you expected when you filed your tax return, you may need to change the amount of tax taken out of your paycheck. The **Withholding Calculator** tool can help you complete a new Form W-4, Employee's Withholding Allowance Certificate to give to your employer.

- **Get Transcript.**

  If you apply for a loan or student financial aid, you may need to get a tax transcript. With **Get Transcript**, you can download and print your transcript or ask the IRS to mail it to your address of record.

- **Interactive Tax Assistant.**

  Use the **Interactive Tax Assistant** tool to get answers to common tax questions. The tool will guide you step-by-step to the answer to your question based on your situation.

- **Tax Map.**

  The **IRS Tax Map** gives you a single point to get tax law information by subject. It integrates your topic with related tax forms, instructions and publications into one research tool.

- **IRS Select Check.**

  If you want to deduct your gift to charity, the organization you give to must be qualified. Use the **IRS Select Check tool** to see if a group is qualified.

And remember, you can always contact Azmoneyguy or your tax professional. They are there to help you save taxes. **Always ask your** advisor before making big financial decisions and to prevent a mistake!

WEEK #39 – The Taxpayer Advocate Service (TAS)

You should know that you have help available, while dealing with the IRS. The Taxpayer Advocate Service (TAS) is the separate department of the Federal Government that is NOT part of the Internal Revenue Service (IRS), even though it is located at an IRS office in major cities of the US.

It is a part of the government that helps taxpayers who have not been treated properly or who are about to lose property or assets from the IRS due to levies, seizures, garnishments, and liens. This might be the last line of defense between you and the IRS, if you do not have a Certified Public Accountant, Enrolled Agent, and attorney representing you.

Taxpayer advocates can stop collection actions under certain conditions, so you can think of them as the "knight in shining armor" coming to your rescue if you follow their rules. The department helps you help yourself. Though there are limits to the TAS abilities, but they can do far more than you can do yourself!

The Taxpayer Advocate Service lists some great tips to educate taxpayers on the type of help it offers:

1. The Taxpayer Advocate Service (TAS) is an independent organization within the IRS and is your voice at the IRS.

2. They help taxpayers whose problems are causing financial difficulty. This includes businesses as well as individuals.

3. You may be eligible for our help if you've tried to resolve your tax problem through normal IRS channels and your issues are still unresolved, or you believe an IRS procedure just isn't working as it should.

4. As a taxpayer, you have rights that the IRS must respect. The IRS has adopted a **Taxpayer Bill of Rights** that includes 10 fundamental rights that every taxpayer has when interacting with the IRS.

   Taxpayer Bill of Rights
   - The Right to Be Informed.
   - The Right to Quality Service.
   - The Right to Pay No More than the Correct Amount of Tax.

- The Right to Challenge the IRS's Position and Be Heard.

- The Right to Appeal an IRS Decision in an Independent Forum.

- The Right to Finality.

- The Right to Privacy.

- The Right to Confidentiality.

- The Right to Retain Representation.

- The Right to a Fair and Just Tax System.

The TAS Tax Toolkit at **TaxpayerAdvocate.irs.gov** can help you understand these rights and what they mean for you. The toolkit also has examples that show how the Taxpayer Bill of Rights can apply in specific situations.

1. If you qualify for TAS help, you'll be assigned to one advocate who will be with you at every turn.

2. The IRS has at least one local taxpayer advocate office in every state, the District of Columbia and Puerto Rico. You can call your advocate, whose number is in your local directory, in **Publication 1546**, Taxpayer Advocate Service - - Your Voice at the IRS, and on our website at **www.irs.gov/advocate**. You can also call us toll-free at 1-877-777- 4778.

3. The TAS tax toolkit at **https://www.taxpayeradvocate.irs.gov** has basic tax information, details about tax credits (for individuals and businesses), and lots more.

4. TAS also handles large-scale or systemic problems that affect many taxpayers.

5. You can get updates at:

   www.facebook.com/YourVoiceAtIRS

   Twitter.com/YourVoiceatIRS

   https://www.youtube.com/tasnta

6. TAS is here to help you because when you're dealing with a tax problem. The worst thing you can do is nothing at all

WEEK #40 – Financial Planning and Fiscal Fitness

Believe it or not, everybody can become a millionaire given enough time. Here's the simple math behind it. Betty and Jonathan taught their son to put away $2,000 into an IRA each year, from the age of ten (10) through twenty (20), and he does no more with the money, but wait.

When Jonathan turns sixty (60) he will have over 1 million dollars with a 6% return. You can replicate this simple rule and your children will thank you because without really having to do much they will have a secured amount, as big as 1 million dollars, waiting for them, when they hit the golden years.

Dreams can be fulfilled, but the first step is to dream and aspire for it. So, you see, everybody can become a millionaire given enough time.

To become a millionaire, consider the following points:

- **Discipline equals success**

  Putting something away each payday is better than waiting until later. Frequently people do not believe they have money to put away. However, if you were to put away the cost of a pack of cigarettes or the money spent on Starbucks each week, you would be surprised to find that you could save many $$ a month.

- **Systematic investing provides the building of wealth**
  Having money taken from your pay and put into a savings account is easy for many people, because they never see the money coming out of their check, they just see their account growing. Everyone needs an emergency fund. An emergency fund should be 3-6 months' worth of living expenses, or a minimum of $1,000. The emergency fund can be placed in a savings account. Even though the interest rate may be low on a savings account, it could save you borrowing a lot of money with a high interest rate, in an emergency.

- **Start today because the longer you wait, the less you make**
  Putting money away when you are 20 is easier than putting it away when you are 40, because you will need to put away three times as much if you wait until 40 to start saving. Compounding allows you to need less at an earlier period, which allows you to have more at a later period.

- **Time and compounding are what make you money**
  Einstein said that the greatest secret in the universe is the power of compounding. Most people become rich from making money on money, not from finding secret stock tips.

The key is investing money in something that pays you money, and then reinvesting it. For instance, buy stocks that pay dividends and then reinvest the dividends. This is better than buying new stocks and hoping they rise drastically over time.

- **Speak with your Financial Advisor (if you do not have one, get one)**

  Discuss what type of savings plan can be established for you. As they say in physics, "An object in motion tends to stay in motion, and an object at rest tends to stay at rest." There are many savings opportunities available and once you start saving, it is easy to continue.

Most of us are aware that we need to have a workout plan to stay physically healthy. Well, believe it or not you also need to have a plan to stay **fiscally** healthy too. So, after learning the theories we listed above on financial planning, let's learn how to develop a specific financial exercise plan to know roughly how much you should be spending on a few different items. This plan is based on an annual basis of spending for the entire year. While some categories spent may be more than the annual range for any one month, if you stay in the range by the end of the year, you should be fine.

You should always have 6 month's living expenses set aside in an Emergency Fund (Not invested, just sitting in a bank or credit union account), before you set about anything else. AND, if you are married or have children you MUST have term life insurance of ten (10) times the breadwinner's annual salary.

After that, then the standard to try to manage is listed below (this is a guide). **For example:**

- **Housing 17-25%** (Rent/mortgage, repairs and escrow (property or renter's insurance and property tax) payments)

- **Food 10-14%** (Includes groceries for yourself and the family only)

- **Transportation 10-13%** (Gas, car payment, repairs, insurance)

- **Entertainment and Clothes 5-9%** (Clothes, movies, theatre, theme parks, gifts to others and holidays)

- **Utilities 5-9%** (Gas, electricity, water and phone)

- **Retirement Account 15%** (This is from your Gross income, and you only do this AFTER you have an emergency fund saved)

- **Healthcare 7-10%**

- **Charity 5-10%** (Ideally 10% is best, but sometimes you must adjust, what you donate to local charities)

Once you get an idea of what your specific spending habits are, you might be able to adjust so that you meet or even beat the average of the American taxpayer.

Additionally, you should have an idea of the priority of spending for these categories (which bills should be paid first, second, third, etc.):

1. Food

2. Housing

3. Utilities

4. Transportation

These are guidelines, and certainly mitigated by each person's circumstances. Remember, not everyone will spend in all the categories listed. Your fiscal exercise plan should be to try and stay within the target ranges each month.

By using the financial planning tips, coupled with the fiscal fitness schedule listed above you should be able to become financially successful and independent quickly. **Like in the story of the tortoise and the hare, the tortoise ALWAYS wins.** Similarly, financial success is not a sprint; it's a long-distance marathon.

5. Healthcare

6. Retirement Account

7. Charity

8. Entertainment or Clothes

WEEK #41 – IRS Urges Travelers Requiring Passports to Pay Their Taxes or Enter into Payment Agreements; (People Owing More than $50,000)

Flying off to an international destination and starting life afresh in an exotic island, is not an option when you have large piling tax debts on you. Not anymore! This idea often glamorized in movies as a fresh start to a new life, is no longer possible for individuals with "seriously delinquent tax debts". The IRS now has updated procedures affecting these individuals, as part of the Fixing America's Surface Transportation (FAST) Act, signed into law in December 2015. The FAST Act requires the IRS to notify the State Department of taxpayers the IRS has certified as owing a seriously delinquent tax debt. See IRS Notice 2018-1. The FAST Act also requires the State Department to deny their passport application or deny renewal of their passport. In some cases, the State Department may revoke their passport.

Taxpayers affected by this law are those with a seriously delinquent tax debt. A taxpayer with a seriously delinquent tax debt is generally someone who owes the IRS more than $50,000 in back taxes, penalties and interest for which the IRS has filed a Notice of Federal

Tax Lien and the period to challenge it has expired, or the IRS has issued a levy.

There are several ways taxpayers can avoid having the IRS notify the State Department of their seriously delinquent tax debt. They include the following:

- Paying the tax debt in full

- Paying the tax debt timely under an approved installment agreement

- Paying the tax debt timely under an accepted offer in compromise

- Paying the tax debt timely under the terms of a settlement agreement with the Department of Justice

- Having requested or have a pending collection due process appeal with a levy

- Having collection suspended because a taxpayer has made an innocent spouse election or requested innocent spouse relief.

And a passport won't be at risk under this program for any taxpayer:

- In bankruptcy proceedings

- Identified by the IRS as a victim of tax-related identity theft

- Whose account the IRS has determined is currently not collectible due to hardship

- Located within a federally declared disaster area

- Pending a request with the IRS, for an installment agreement payment plan

- With a pending Offer in Compromise with the IRS

- With an IRS accepted adjustment that will satisfy the debt in full

For taxpayers serving in a combat zone who owe a seriously delinquent tax debt, the IRS postpones collection and notifies the State Department and the individual's passport is not subject to denial during this time.

In general, taxpayers behind on their tax obligations should come forward and pay what they owe or enter a payment plan with the IRS.

Frequently, taxpayers qualify for one of several relief programs, including the following:

- Can request a payment agreement with the IRS by filing **Form 9465**. Taxpayers can download this form from IRS.gov and mail it along with a tax return, bill or notice. Some taxpayers can use the online payment agreement to set up a monthly payment agreement for up to 72 months.

- Some financially distressed taxpayers may qualify for an **Offer in Compromise**. This is an agreement between a taxpayer and the IRS that settles the taxpayer's tax liabilities for less than the full amount owed. The IRS looks at the taxpayer's income and assets to determine the taxpayer's ability to pay. To help determine eligibility, use the Offer in Compromise Pre-Qualifier, a free online tool available on **https://www.irs.gov/.**

WEEK #42 – Tips for U.S. Taxpayers with Foreign Income

It's not like 'Out of sight, out of mind'. You can't do that with the taxes you owe to your country of residence or origin. While you work abroad for a foreign company (or an American company with a foreign headquarters), you might be eligible for some tax advantages when you live and work abroad.

So, even if you live or work abroad or receive income from foreign sources during the year, being a U.S. citizen or resident, you must report income from all sources within and outside of the country. The rules for filing income tax returns are generally the same, whether you're living in the U.S. or overseas.

Here are seven tips from the IRS that U.S. taxpayers with foreign income should know:

1. **Report Worldwide Income.**

    By law, U.S. citizens and resident aliens must report their worldwide income. This includes income from foreign trusts, and foreign bank and securities accounts.

2. File Required Tax Forms.

You may need to file Schedule B, Interest and Ordinary Dividends, with your U.S. tax return. You may also need to file **Form 8938**, Statement of Specified Foreign Financial Assets. In some cases, you may need to file FinCEN Form 114, Report of Foreign Bank and Financial Accounts. See Azmoneyguy or your tax advisor for more information.

3. Consider the Automatic Extension.

If you're living abroad and can't file your return by the April 15 deadline, you probably qualify for an automatic extension until June 15. This is available to taxpayers who are living outside the US. You'll then have additional time to file your U.S. income tax return.

4. Review the Foreign Earned Income Exclusion.

If you live and work abroad, you may be able to claim the foreign earned income exclusion. If you qualify, you won't pay tax on wages earned outside the US and other foreign earned income. Each year the Foreign Income Exclusion amount changes. See your tax advisor for the current exclusion amount. For even more information, see instructions on **Form 2555**, Foreign Earned Income.

5. Don't Overlook Credits and Deductions.

You may be able to take either a tax credit or a deduction (but not both) for income taxes you paid to a foreign country. These benefits can reduce the amount of taxes you must pay if both countries tax the same income.

6. Get Tax Help Outside the U.S.

The IRS has offices in Frankfurt, London, Paris and Beijing. IRS staff at these offices can help you with tax filing issues and answer your tax questions.

WEEK #43 –Tax Tips for New Businesses and Self-Employed Taxpayers

Josephine perfected the art of baking. Her cookies, cakes and pies were always a hit amongst friends and family who persuaded her to take it up professionally. Encouraged by them, Josephine started a bakery specializing in hand-made and hand-crafted products. While her venture was a success, because the result was baked with love, what she was struggling with was understanding her tax dues.

America is a free country, promoting entrepreneurial growth, even more so with the current tax laws. So, if you start a business, like Josephine, you need to know about your federal tax obligations and opportunities that are available. You may need to know not only about income taxes, but also about payroll taxes.

Here are five basic tax tips that can help get your business off to a good start:

1. **Business Structure.**

    As you start out, you'll need to **choose the structure of your business**. Some common types include sole proprietorship, partnership and corporation. You may also choose to be an S corporation or Limited Liability Company (LLC). You'll report your business activity using the IRS forms which are right for your business type.

2. **Business Taxes.**

There are four general types of business taxes. They are income tax, self-employment tax, employment tax and excise tax. The type of taxes your business pays usually depends on which type of business you choose to set up. You may need to pay your taxes by making estimated tax payments.

3. **Employer Identification Number (EIN).**

You may need to get an EIN for federal tax purposes. Search "do you need an EIN" on IRS.gov to find out if you need this number. If you do need one, you can apply for it online, and it's free to do so, if you do it yourself. You must apply online, Monday thru Friday and be sure to do so, 8am – 5pm Eastern Time (ET).

4. **Accounting Method.**

An accounting method is a set of rules that determine when to report income and expenses. Your business must use a consistent method. The two that are most common are the **cash method** and the **accrual method**. Under the cash method, you normally report income in the year that you receive it and deduct expenses in the year that you pay them. Under the accrual method, you generally report income in the

240

year that you earn it, (regardless of how long it takes for clients to pay you) and deduct expenses in the year that you incur them (regardless of how long it takes for you to pay vendors). This is true, even if you receive the income or pay the expenses in a future year.

5. **Employee Health Care.**

The Small Business Health Care Tax Credit helps small businesses and tax-exempt organizations pay for health care coverage they offer their employees. A small employer is eligible for the credit, if it has fewer than 25 employees who work full-time, or a combination of full-time and part-time. Beginning in 2014, the maximum credit is 50 percent of premiums paid for small business employers and 35 percent of premiums paid for small tax-exempt employers, such as charities since 2017, employers employing at least a certain number of employees (generally 50 full- time employees or a combination of full-time and part-time employees that is equivalent to 50 full-time employees) will be subject to the Employer Shared Responsibility provision.

Tips for Self-Employed Taxpayers

If you are an independent contractor or run your own business, there are a few basic things to know when it comes to your federal tax return.

Here are some tips from the IRS, you should know about income from self-employment:

1. Self-employment income can include income you received for part-time work. This is in addition to income from your regular job.

2. You must file a **Schedule C**, Profit or Loss from Business, or **Schedule C-EZ**, Net Profit from Business, with your Form 1040.

3. You may have to pay self-employment tax as well as income tax if you made a profit. Self- employment tax includes Social Security and Medicare taxes. Use **Schedule SE**, Self-Employment Tax, to figure the tax. Make sure to file the schedule with your tax return.

4. You may need to make estimated tax payments. People typically make these payments on income that is not subject to withholding. You may be charged a penalty if you do not pay enough taxes throughout the year.

5. You can deduct expenses you paid to run your trade or business. You can deduct most business expenses in full, but

some must be '**capitalized**.' This means you must depreciate (write off) the expense over a period of years.

6. You can deduct business costs only if they are both ordinary and necessary. An ordinary expense is one that is common and accepted in your industry. A necessary expense is one that is helpful and proper for your trade or business.

7. You may be able to hire your children to assist you in your occupation and receive a tax business deduction for paying them wages to help you. Also, their wages may not be taxable under certain conditions.

8. You can deduct health insurance premiums (including Medicare) on your personal tax return without itemizing

9. You may be eligible for the Qualified Business Income Deduction of up to 20% of your profits as a business deduction since 2018.

Home Office Deductions

If you work from home, you should learn the rules for how to claim the home office deduction. Today, a simplified option is available to figure the deduction for business use of your home. The new option may save you time because it simplifies how you figure and claim the deduction. It can also make it easier for you to keep records. It does not change the rules for who may claim the deduction.

Here are six tips from the IRS about the home office deduction:

1. Generally, in order to claim a deduction for a home office, you must use a part of your home exclusively and regularly for business purposes. Also, the part of your home used for business must be:

   - Your principal place of business, or
   - A place where you meet clients or customers in the normal course of business, or
   - A separate structure not attached to your home. Examples might include a studio, garage or barn.

2. If you use the actual expense method, the home office deduction includes certain costs that you paid for your home. For example, if you rent your home, part of the rent you paid could qualify. If you own your home, part of the mortgage interest, taxes and utilities you paid could qualify. The amount you can deduct usually depends on the percentage of your home used for business.

3. Beginning with 2013 tax returns, you may be able to use the simplified option to claim the home office deduction instead of claiming actual expenses. Under this method, you multiply the allowable square footage of your office by a prescribed rate of $5.

The maximum footage allowed is 300 square feet. The deduction limit using this method is $1,500 per year.

4. If your gross income from the business use of your home is less than your expenses, the deduction for some expenses may be limited.

5. If you are self-employed and choose the actual expense method, use **Form 8829**, Expenses for Business Use of Your Home, to figure the amount you can deduct. You claim your deduction on **Schedule C**, Profit or Loss from Business, if you use either the simplified or actual expense method. See the Schedule C instructions for how to report your deduction.

6. If you are an employee, you must meet additional rules to claim the deduction. For example, in addition to the above tests, your business use must also be for your employer's convenience.

WEEK #44 – Casualty, Theft and Disaster Losses

Hurricanes Harvey, Irma, Jose and Maria all made their impact felt back to back. Images of flooded streets, devastated homes and shattered families tugged at your heart. The year 2017 witnessed many disasters nationwide that spurred Congress to pass the "Disaster Tax Relief and Airport and Airway Extension Act". Due to this Act, many changes have occurred that greatly benefit taxpayers who experience disaster losses.

Rebecca's family of six, residing in Houston, was severely affected by the category 4 storm that hit Texas. They lost their house and many valuables. While monetary compensation can never make up for their loss, but it can at least help them in slowly regaining normalcy, especially after the crippling effect of the devastating disasters.

If you experience damage from a storm, theft, auto wreck, fire, flood, earthquake, break in, terrorist event or other disaster, you need to contact the police and your insurance company. Once you file a claim, your next step is to total the amount of your losses. After your insurance company reimburses you (if any), your Casualty Loss is what is left over.

The tax relief or benefit of a casualty loss is an Ordinary Tax Loss on your tax return and provides tax relief that may **PAY YOU** in your time of need. This type of loss is an additional tax deduction, on top of any standard deduction you might take, and adds extra expenses to any itemized deductions. While the disaster is terrible and may be devastating at the time, it's heartening to know that the IRS gives you some relief on any taxes you might otherwise pay.

If the disaster is in a Federal Declared Disaster Area or Zone, you will also qualify for a delay of time on when your tax returns and tax payments must be filed or paid. Each disaster will have different time frames, but you could get up to an **extra year** to have to file returns. See Azmoneyguy or your tax professional for these time specifics. Another relief you can benefit from is that if you need to withdraw funds from your retirement account, you **will not** be hit with an early withdrawal penalty! This will save you 10% of what you have withdrawn (that's the amount of the early withdrawal penalty, normally).

Those taxpayers who might be able to claim Earned Income Tax Credit or Child Tax Credit (EITC and CTC) also receive some relief, for the disaster tax year. As an example, individuals affected by Hurricanes Harvey, Irma and Maria, who earned less income in 2017 than 2016, can use the 2016 amounts reported, to claim EITC or CTC in 2017.

Also, you might be able to take the current loss backward and amend your past tax returns for immediate refunds. For example, a loss that occurs in 2019 can be listed on your amended 2018 tax return, so that you can immediately file for a refund and use the money to help you get back on your feet. Use IRS forms 4684 and 1040X to amend past returns. Or you may use the amount of your disaster loss on your current year tax return, on IRS form 4684 if it has not been filed yet.

It is possible for a casualty loss to use up all income for the past year, plus your current year. This is known as a Net Operating Loss (NOL). If the loss is large enough, you may have no taxes for the past year, the current year, or some future years, depending on how great the loss is compared to your income. If casualty losses exceed your income, you have a loss in that year and could pay no taxes. And you get to carry excess losses backwards or forwards, to help you get back on your feet.

Here are some things to remember:

- **Losses can occur for many reasons: theft, fire, storm, auto wreck, earthquake, terrorist event and other sudden disasters**

- **The amount of the loss, after insurance reimbursement, is your Casualty Loss deduction**

- You can amend your prior years' tax returns for the current loss you experienced (File IRS forms 4684 and 1040X), or you can use the Casualty Loss in the current year (your choice)

- You may qualify for delayed time to both file returns and pay taxes up to a year after the normal due date.

- Money withdrawn from retirement accounts will not get hit with the early withdrawal penalty (10% of the amount withdrawn, usually)

- Those who qualified for EITC and CTC in the past year, might be able to use that income amount for the current year, to qualify again for extra refunds

- If the amount of loss is great enough to absorb all your income, you have a Net Operating Loss (NOL) and you can carry the loss forward into future years, until the loss is used (investments that were stolen by Bernie Madoff in 2008 were carried backward and/or forward if it exceeded current incomes). These losses helped some taxpayers to not pay taxes for many years, depending on each person's circumstances.

For 2018 thru 2025, only disasters declared by the President, qualify for tax relief, stated above. Go to https://www.fema.gov/ and make sure your state had a declared disaster for the year you are filing for.

Robert F Hockensmith

WEEK #45 — Military Tax Benefits

You have sacrificed your youth, precious time, and the warmth of family to keep not only Americans, but at times citizens from across the world safe. You deserve more than admiration and gratitude. It's that time of the year, when we honor our veterans. Since its almost Veteran's Day, so let's discuss some of the tax benefits for the U.S. military forces. Some types of pay are not taxable. And special rules may apply to some tax deductions, credits and deadlines.

These rules apply to all branches of U.S. Armed Forces, whether they are National Guard, Reserves, or Active Duty:

- **Filing tax returns late**

  Service members have up to the later of 180 days after returning from a combat zone deployment, or combat related hospital stay, to file tax returns without late penalties or interest. Military members have until June 15th to file returns if they are overseas and not in a combat zone.

- **Combat Pay Exclusion**

  If you serve in a combat zone, certain **combat pay is not taxable**. You won't need to show the pay on your tax return because combat pay isn't included in the wages reported on your Form W-2, Wage and Tax Statement. Service in support of a combat zone may qualify for this exclusion.

- **Qualified Reservist Distributions and Repayments**
  Reservists who are called into active service, may be able to take distributions from retirement accounts (IRA, 401K, TSP, etc.) without penalty and may also repay any distributions taken, even if the repayment exceeds the annual IRA contribution limit. This is like borrowing from a 401K and paying it back. Certain conditions apply, ask Azmoneyguy or your tax professional.

- **Selling a Home for tax purposes and getting the Capital Gain Exclusion**
  Time deployed counts for the five-year living at the same address rule, to help sell the home and avoid Capital Gains. You must live in your home 2 of 5 years to get Capital Gains Exclusion.

- **Overnight Travel Expenses for National Guard and Reserve members living more than 100 miles from duty station**
  This deduction is on the front of the tax return, and no itemizing is required. This allows you to write off travel, lodging, and meal expenses.

- **Deductions for Uniforms, Equipment and Laundry**

  You can write off uniforms you purchase, or any repairs made to them, as well as the cost of laundering the uniforms, plus any military equipment you purchase for your use. There are special rules that allow military personnel to even deduct the cost for laundry and haircuts, if away from home for less than one year on temporary duty.

- **Some states offer little or no state tax on military members and spouse's earnings**

  Arizona and many other states have no tax on military pay, and no tax on the spouse's earnings either. You can claim residence in any state if you are on active duty in the military. For instance, you can be stationed in Ft. Huachuca, Arizona and still claim a Nevada residency. This means you would not have to prepare an Arizona tax return, if you are active military. This would allow you to not pay state taxes to the State of Arizona even while you are stationed and living in Arizona. This also counts for vehicle registration tax. Be sure to check on the laws of the state you are living in for your situation with Azmoneyguy or your tax professional.

- **Military allowances are tax-free**

  Some examples of allowances would be Clothing Allowance, Family Separation Allowance, Base Housing Allowance, Per

Diem Allowance, and Temporary Duty Allowance. These are all monies that are given to you in addition to your regular payroll that is not subject to tax.

- **Forgiveness of tax upon Death**

  Current year, previous year and unpaid taxes are forgiven and/or refunded when military members die, if they are active duty during either a terrorist event, in a combat zone, or in support of a military combat action.

- **Earned Income Tax Credit (EITC)**

  If you get nontaxable combat pay, you may choose to include it to figure your EITC. You will make this choice only if it increases your credit. Even if you do, the combat pay stays nontaxable.

- **Signing Joint Returns**

  Both spouses normally must sign a joint income tax return. If your spouse is absent due to certain military duty or conditions, you may be able to sign for your spouse, by attaching a copy of the military combat orders. In other cases when your spouse is absent, you may need an IRS power of attorney to file a joint return.

- **Moving Expenses**

  Members of the military still get to take a deduction for the out of pocket costs of moving household goods and family members, to include pets, for any costs not already paid for or reimbursed by the military.

WEEK #46 - What to Do If You Win the Lottery Or Big In Vegas?

"Someday . . . if I win the lottery!" Aren't we all harboring a thought like this in some tiny corner of our heart? Yes, many of us hope to win the Lottery at some point in our lives. Who can deny the charm of a fancy glamorous life, without really having to work hard for it? What if the Powerball winning number matches this time, or if you win, in the casino, playing Blackjack?

We dream of the easy life, and being able to buy whatever we want without worrying about the cost, but what are some of the tax ramifications of such a windfall? Whether it's the lottery, a pool at work, keno, scratchers or some other game of chance, there are a few ways to keep more of what you win and pay the tax man less.

If you're a casual gambler, odds are good that these basic tax tips can help you at tax time next year:

1. **Gambling income**

    Gambling income includes winnings from lotteries, horse racing and casinos. It also includes cash prizes and the fair market value of prizes like cars and trips.

2. Payer tax form

If you win, you may get a Form W-2G, Certain Gambling Winnings, from the payer. The IRS also gets a copy of the W-2G. The payer issues the form depending on the type of game you played, the amount of your winnings and other factors. You'll also get the form if the payer withholds taxes from what you won.

3. How to report winnings

You must report all your gambling winnings as income. This is true even if you don't receive a Form W-2G. You normally report your winnings for the year on your tax return as 'other income.'

4. How to deduct losses

You can deduct your gambling losses on Schedule A, Itemized Deductions. The amount you can deduct is limited to the amount of the gambling income you report on your return.

5. Keep gambling receipts to save, if you win later

You should keep track of your wins and losses. This includes keeping items such as a gambling log or diary, receipts, statements or tickets. Often, once players find out they did NOT win, people simply throw the losing tickets away.

WRONG!! You may not win today but keep all those losing tickets until the end of the year as proof that you lost. This, because you can reduce any winnings that year against any losses you incur until the end of the year. Then you start over again next year. Consider throwing away $1,000 worth of losing tickets, and then at the end of the year, you win $3000. You will pay taxes overall $3,000 unless you kept the losing tickets. Keeping these losing tickets lets you reduce your winnings and your tax bill. For most people that's about a $300 tax savings.

6. **Seek professional advice**

    If you win the BIG one, always see a good accountant and attorney BEFORE you tell anyone about the win. These professionals can give you some excellent advice before going public.

7. **Consider a Partnership Strategy for ownership of tickets**

    If you buy a ticket as a member of a group or family, consider a Limited Partnership strategy to be the entity that owns the winning ticket, rather than one person. This is a great way to reduce taxes by spreading the wealth as they say around the family or group, because many in the group will be at different tax brackets.

8. Decide which payout option to use

Consider whether to take the cash payout or the 20-year payout. For older winners, the cash payout may be best, but then again, maybe a 20-year payout might be a form of protection for your heirs. Again, seek professional advice BEFORE collecting your winnings.

Here are some points to remember:

1. **Keep your playing tickets until year end** (in case you win later)

2. **Seek professional assistance** (CPA, EA or Attorney)

3. **Consider a partnership to own the winning ticket**

4. **Decide which pay out option is best for you** (immediate cash payout or an annuity payment over many years)

WEEK #47 – Money Savings and Tax Tips for the Holidays

The Holiday Season is finally here. The bright red ornaments, Santa himself and the dazzling colorful gift-wrapped parcels sitting almost everywhere in town surely entices you to indulge in the holiday spirit. The holidays are upon us. It should be a pleasant time, but too often the enjoyment we experience is followed by financial stress, worries and/or headache.

Money Savings Tips

January's bank statements and credit card statements bring the realization that once again, we have lost control of our spending habits and busted our budget. Who says we shouldn't enjoy? We should enjoy the holiday spirit but remember that enjoying does not necessarily translate into overspending.

Before the holidays begin, you should consider making a budget. Estimate the cost of what you plan to buy, and if the total cost is manageable, then stick firmly to it as you shop. If it's not, then look for ways to cut back.

Typically, use the rule of thumb: **YOUR CREDIT CARD BILL FOR THE HOLIDAYS SHOULD BE PAID OFF IN 90 DAYS.** If it takes more than 90 days to pay your holiday credit card off, that means you spent more than you should have.

Consider ways to save on holiday gifts:

1. Many families can draw names and give one nice gift to a person rather than multiple small ones.
2. Make or bake gifts instead of buying them.
3. Give combined gifts from parents or children instead of individuals.
4. Agree with your close friends on a spending limit.

The holidays are a special time for children, too. But here, you must curb your excesses, so you can teach your children lessons on spending. Remember, you don't have to give children every gift they want.

1. When they make a holiday list, have them prioritize the things they want.
2. Don't forget, favored toys are often simple toys that allow them to use their imagination.
3. Show your children there is more to the holidays than simply receiving presents.
4. Have them participate in choosing and wrapping presents for a less fortunate child.
5. Encourage them to make their own gifts for families and friends.

6. Arrange family outings and fun activities, so the holidays become a series of joyful events.

Here are some things to remember:

- **Set a budget** (credit cards should be paid off in 90 days)

- **Save on gifts** (buy one nice gift instead of multiple small gifts)

- **Make or bake gifts instead of buying them**

- **Give combined gifts from parents or children**

- **Teach your children how to participate in the holidays** (have them choose or wrap gifts for a less fortunate child)

- **Have children make their own gifts for family or friends**

Tax Tips for Holidays

Holiday Meal Deductions are worth 100% deductions (2018 and later)

It's that time of the year when the spirit of giving is at its hilt. The holiday season of spreading joy and good cheer is here and this is the best time to discuss some little known or used tax deductions that are available for the business owner during the holiday season.

Typically, if an employer or owner of a small business takes employees out to lunch, or pays for a gift like a birthday, graduation, wedding, anniversary, baptism, or bar (bat) mitzvah, then there is only a 50% tax deduction for the cost of the meal, entertainment and/or gift.

So, if an employer/owner purchases a small **HOLIDAY** gift such as a turkey, ham, or bottle of wine, half of the costs of the purchase is allowed. The only things that need to be proven to receive this 100% tax deduction, are the date, place, purpose and dollar amount spent. This will allow the company or business owner the opportunity to write off the deduction at 100%.

The IRS does not define what holidays are allowed for this deduction. So, whether you are Christian, Muslim, Jewish, or belong to any other faith, you should be able to justify a holiday meal at 100% deduction for a business that is paying for it. You are eligible to benefit from it if you are self- employed, with employees, or own a corporation and you are an employee as well.

Here are some things to remember:

- **Holiday meals are fully deductible** (100% write off)

- **Small holiday gifts that are given are deductible to the employer or business owner** (ham, turkey, wine)

- **The documentation that is required to claim the total deduction is the date, purpose of meal or gift, place of meal or gift and the dollar amount**

WEEK #48 - Business Use of Personal Vehicle

Downtown, uptown, residential areas . . . you happen to see them all back and forth, so many times, all in a day. Chances are, you are in a profession that practically makes you live in your vehicle. Seems your vehicle has basically become an office on wheels.

It's also a tax deduction, if you structure it correctly. Karen, a marketing manager by profession knows that you can deduct auto expenses when you own or lease a personal vehicle and use it for business purposes. For instance, making deliveries, traveling to and from meetings, trips to the office supply store, your bank, clients, and so forth are considered a business deduction.

Commuting, on the other hand, going back and forth from home to work, is not a deduction.

You have two different ways of calculating a business deduction for a vehicle: **The Actual Expense Method or Standard Mileage Method.** And both methods require you keep a logbook.

If you choose the **Standard Mileage Method**, all you need to do is keep a logbook of both business and personal miles driven, and a record of any parking fees, tolls, or auto license tag expenses. While the Standard Mileage Rate is usually easier to track, you must still record the date, mileage driven, names, and relationships of clients, and business location for each trip. Multiply the business miles driven by the standard mileage rate and that is your deduction, including any expenses for parking fees, tolls, and auto license tags. Today there are many smartphone apps available to keep track of your mileage from your smartphone GPS.

Alternately, if you use the **Actual Expense Method**, you still must keep a logbook for your business miles versus your personal miles and all information listed above. Along with it, under the Actual Expense Method, you must keep track of maintenance, gas, tires, insurance, interest expense on loans, and other expenses out of pocket. You even get a tax deduction for depreciation on your vehicle depending on the business use of that vehicle.

Which method is best?

Keep track of the logbook and figure it out using both methods to see which one gives you the better deduction.

The caveat is, once you've used the Actual Expense Method, you are stuck using that method until you trade vehicles. Further, if you use the Actual Expense Method, you must take depreciation for the business use and you may have to recapture the depreciation when you dispose of the vehicle. Be sure you can prove that your business use of a personal vehicle is MORE THAN 50% or you will have to revert to the mileage method for that vehicle.

Business Owned Vehicles

Autos and trucks owned and titled to the business name do NOT need logbooks kept IF you park the vehicles at the office location, when not in use and the vehicles are not used by employees for personal use or taken home at night.

This rule does not apply if you have a home office. You are still required to keep logbooks, because the Internal Revenue Service (IRS) uses a "first call last call" rule to compensate for reduced commuting by owner-employees.

The first call (trip) and the last call (trip) you make each day will be considered commuting and not deductible.

Also, interest on auto loans and auto tags paid are tax deductible for businesses whether they use Standard Mileage or Actual Expense methods.

Here are some points to remember:

- **Two methods for vehicle deduction: Actual Expense versus Standard Mileage**
- **Both methods require a logbook to keep track of business versus personal mileage and reason for trips** (Consider smartphone apps that track your mileage)
- **The best method is the one that gives you the biggest deduction; but there are some drawbacks to both**

(depreciation recapture and possible reduced deduction on converting actual to mileage)

- **With either method, you also get to write off your license plates if you itemize on your tax return**

WEEK #49 – Carryover Option for Health Flexible Spending Arrangements (FSA)

As, they say health is wealth! So even in matters of wealth, health gains some prominence. The IRS offers some carryover to health flexible spending arrangements (FSAs). The carryover can be advantageous, but like all IRS rules this one is complicated. There are some important limitations you need to know before taking advantage of a Health Flexible Spending Arrangement.

Nancy, a Human Resources (HR) professional knows that employers may allow plan participants to carry over up to $500 of their unused health FSA balances remaining at the end of a plan year, to the next year. But you must also understand, this choice or feature is not mandatory for an employer, it is optional. It is also an alternative to offering a grace period (waiting period), as many employers already do. Employers can offer the carryover, the grace period, or nothing.

Health FSA's are common benefits under employer-sponsored cafeteria plans. A health FSA may be credited or funded with employer contributions or pre-tax employee salary reductions. Health FSA dollars can be used for a variety of qualified medical expenses including, but not limited to, the cost of chiropractors, dental or vision expenses, over-the-counter medicines or drugs if a prescription has been obtained. Amounts in a health FSA at the end of the plan year generally cannot be carried over to the next year. This is known as the "Use it or lose it" rule.

In 2013, the IRS noted that health FSA's were not utilized to their fullest extent because the use- or-lose rule was the greatest hurdle. Many taxpayers cannot predict their future needs for medical expenses and are reluctant to open a health FSA for fear of forfeiting the unused funds. Moreover, in 2017, the Affordable Care Act put a $2,600 cap on allowable annual contributions, further stressing participants to manage their FSA dollars carefully. So, the IRS announced a change to the use-or-lose rule in 2013.

Today, an employer may amend its cafeteria plan to provide for the carryover to the immediately following year of up to $500 of any amount remaining unused as of the end of the year in a health FSA. The carryover does not count against or otherwise affect the $2,600 salary reduction limit (adjusted for inflation after 2017) for health FSAs applicable to each plan year.

The IRS set $500 as the maximum carryover amount. As mentioned earlier, an employer also may choose to do nothing and not offer the carryover option.

Here are some things to remember:

- FSA's are employer options (cafeteria plans) offered to employees.

- Contributions to FSA can be made by either or both, employees or employers.

- Contributions made to an employee benefit plan are tax free.

- Money used by FSA accounts is for medical, dental or vision expenses.

- Employees that use FSA accounts must use or lose the amount contributed to the plan by year end or lose the money left over.

- There is an exception that allows up to $500 of money in employee's Accounts to be carried over to the next year.

Robert F Hockensmith

WEEK # 50 – Year End Tax Savings and Deductions

Even if you have not been systematic about financial planning since the beginning of the year, it's heartening to know that it's never too late. You can jump into this marathon of financial planning whenever you want to, but like all healthy habits, the earlier you start the better it is for your own good.

Since, year-end is right around the corner so we'll discuss about some things that we can do towards the end of the year to save on our taxes and maximize our deductions.

- **Make HSA contributions.**

  A Health Savings Account (HSA) is for people who may be eligible to put away $7,000* each year. And if you are 55 years old, or older, you can put away an additional $1,000. This is a tax deduction for your business if you are self-employed, or if you are an employee that is eligible for an HSA, it could be a tax personal tax deduction as well.

- **If employed, be sure to fund IRA retirement accounts.**

  Retirement accounts such as an IRA allow you to put away as much as $6,000*, if you are under 50 years old. You can put away as much as $7,000* if you are 50 years old or older. This is allowed if you or your spouse earns at least $7,000*. If you earn nothing and your spouse earns $15,000* you would both be eligible to put up to $7,000* each into an IRA account. You may also choose to contribute to a Roth IRA. This will not help you with current taxes, but it will save you future taxes because any money left in a Roth IRA is tax-free after 5 years.

- **If you are self-employed, set up a Keogh Plan, 401K, or Solo-K (1-2-person retirement plan) and fund them to maximize tax savings.**

  You can also put money into a Simple IRA, SEP IRA, or a Solo 401K, which is a retirement account for an owner and/or owner's spouse. Keogh's let you put away up to 25% of your earnings (limited) while 401k's allow up to $56,000*, depending on your age and income. SEP IRA's let you put away up to $56,000*, while Simple IRA's allow you to put away as much as $13,000*, if under 50 or $16,000* if 50 or older. Don't forget that many employers match retirement plan contributions up to certain limits and the IRS offers a tax credit for new savers, for both employers & employees.

- **Don't hold off on Energy Saving Home Improvements*.**

  Energy saving home improvements such as exterior doors, windows, air conditioners, water heaters, and solar devices allow you an opportunity to save on federal taxes, and some states may offer state tax credits as well. A tax credit is a reduction on your taxes, while a deduction reduces your taxable income. Typically, $1 in tax credit may be equivalent to $3 in tax deductions. It is far better to receive a tax credit than a tax deduction. The SECURE Act kept this credit in place.

- **Use IRA's to make charitable contributions**

  You can take money out of your IRA for a charitable contribution, which means you effectively get a tax-free withdrawal from your IRA if the amount of the charitable contribution, is the amount of your IRA distribution. You can donate up to $100,000 and get a tax deduction for the contribution, and not pay taxes on the distribution.

- **Divorces**

  Any alimony payments for divorces decreed **after** 2018 will **not** be tax deductible. Any divorces decreed **prior** to 2019 still allow alimony payments as a deduction, but you must now list the date of the divorce on the tax return, along with the recipient's name address, social security number and amount paid to ex-spouse.

These are available for 2019, be sure to check with your tax advisor for current amounts.

Robert F Hockensmith

WEEK #51 - Tax Tips about Hobbies and a Home Office from the Internal Revenue Service (IRS)

From a small wooden box in a corner of your room, to a coveted wall in your study, they have grown with you. You have them from all over the world like Japan, China, Spain, Portugal, Ghana, Morocco and the like. Your collection of stamps is enviable! That's what hobbies do to you. They grow with you and drive you to passionately increase your collection- be it of stamps, coins, flowers or any other object of interest. If you enjoy any hobby like stamp collecting, fishkeeping, gardening, sculpting, horsemanship and the like, and your hobby is also a source of income, then you must report the income you earn from your hobby on your tax return.

The rules for how you report the income and expenses depend on whether the activity is a hobby or a business. There are special rules and limits for deductions you can claim for a hobby.

Here are five tax tips you should know about hobbies:

1. **Is it a Business or a Hobby?**

    A key feature of a business is that you do it to make a profit. You often engage in a hobby for sport or recreation, not to make a profit. You should consider the IRS nine factors:
    - You carry on the activity in a businesslike manner
    - The time and effort you put into the activity indicate that you intend to make it profitable
    - You depend on income from the activity for your livelihood
    - Your losses are due to circumstances beyond your control, or are normal in the startup phase of your type of business
    - You adjust your methods of operation to improve profitability
    - You (or your advisors) have the knowledge needed to carry on the activity as a successful business
    - You were successful in making a profit in similar activities in the past
    - The activity makes a profit in some years, and how much profit it makes
    - You can expect to make a future profit from the appreciation of the assets used in the activity when you determine whether your activity is a hobby.

Make sure to base your determination on all the facts and circumstances of your situation. For more about business rules see **Publication 535**, Business Expenses, or contact Azmoneyguy or your tax professional.

2. **Allowable Hobby Deductions.**

   Within certain limits, you can usually deduct ordinary and necessary hobby expenses. An ordinary expense is one that is common and accepted for the activity. A necessary expense is one that is appropriate for the activity.

3. **Limits on Hobby Expenses.**

   Generally, you can only deduct your hobby expenses up to the amount of hobby income. If your hobby expenses are more than your hobby income, you have a loss from the activity. You can't deduct the loss from your other income.

4. **How to Deduct Hobby Expenses.**

   You must itemize deductions on your tax return in order to deduct hobby expenses. Your expenses may fall into three types of deductions, and special rules apply to each type. See Publication 535, Azmoneyguy or your tax professional for the rules about how you claim them.

5. Use IRS Free File.

Hobby rules can be complex and **IRS Free File** can make filing your tax return easier. IRS Free File is available until Oct. 15. If you make $66,000 or less, you can use brand-name tax software. If you earn more, you can use Free File Fillable Forms, an electronic version of IRS paper forms. Free File is available only through the **https://www.irs.gov/** website.

Home Office Deductions

If you work from home, you should learn the rules for how to claim the home office deduction. Since 2013, when the Home Office Act was signed, a simpler option was created to figure the deduction for business use of your home. The new option may save you time because it simplifies how you figure and claim the deduction. It can also make it easier for you to keep records. It does not change the rules for who may claim the deduction.

Here are six tips from the IRS about the home office deduction:

1. Generally, in order to claim a deduction for a home office, you must use a part of your home exclusively and regularly for business purposes. Also, the part of your home used for business must be:

    - Your principal place of business, or

- A place where you meet clients or customers in the normal course of business, or

- A separate structure not attached to your home. Examples might include a studio, garage or barn.

1. If you use the actual expense method, the home office deduction includes certain costs that you paid for your home. For example, if you rent your home, part of the rent you paid could qualify. If you own your home, part of the mortgage interest, taxes and utilities you paid could qualify. The amount you can deduct usually depends on the percentage of your home used for business.

2. You may be able to use the simplified option to claim the home office deduction instead of claiming actual expenses. Under this method, you multiply the allowable square footage of your office by a prescribed rate of $5. The maximum footage allowed is 300 square feet. The deduction limit using this method is $1,500 per year.

3. If your gross income from the business use of your home is less than your expenses, the deduction for some expenses may be limited.

4. If you are self-employed and choose the actual expense method, use **Form 8829**, Expenses for Business Use of Your Home, to figure the amount you can deduct. You claim your deduction on **Schedule C**, Profit or Loss from Business, if you use either the simplified or actual expense method. See the Schedule C instructions for how to report your deduction.

5. Since 2018, employees no longer can write off Employee Business Expenses. You should work with your employer to get a reimbursement for out of pocket expenses, you might spend to complete your job. **Even if the employer reduces your pay for any reimbursement, you would still be better off.** There are no taxes AT ALL, for the amount reimbursed by your employer! Even the employer wins, since there are payroll taxes on the amounts reimbursed either! WIN WIN!

WEEK #52 – Distributions from Retirement Accounts

Sitting by the bonfire, with your favorite drink in hand as you ponder about the year gone by and look forward to the upcoming New Year, your finances and how you plan them surely deserve some mindshare, amongst the clutter of other precious thoughts. While thinking of the immediate and long-term needs, you always want to ensure that you have a well-planned retirement to secure your golden years.

Francis, a banker by profession, had his way with numbers. He knew that knowing your taxes was important to grow your wealth. He knows for those who are nearing the age of seventy (72), there is a little-known tax law called the **Required Minimum Distribution** (RMD). If you have money put away in IRAs, 401ks, or other retirement accounts, after you reach the age of 72 years old, money must be distributed from these retirement plans, annually.

The Internal Revenue Service requires that distributions be taken, at least, every year once you reach the age of 72 years old. You can wait until April 1st. of the year after you reach 72, to take your RMD, but there are some complications with taking a distribution that late. If you do choose this, you will be required to take two distributions in that year to make up for the distribution that you passed up at age 72.

How much to take out of your retirement plans depends on many factors:

1. Your marital status

2. The difference in age of the spouses if you are married – if there is a ten year or more difference in age, a different table is used to compute the RMD

3. Compute the total amount of all retirement plans, divide it by the factor or number on the mortality table the Internal Revenue Service uses, and this determines what your annual RMD should be

4. Repeat steps 1 – 3 annually

   For many taxpayers, the value of your retirement accounts will change every year. The value as of December 31st of the previous year is the number that is used to compute the RMD for the current year. (Example: You must compute the total for all your retirement accounts as of December 31, 2019, to help determine what must be distributed by December 31, 2020.)

This distribution can be taken out at any time during the year. It is preferred to take money out every month, in order to not be hit with penalties at year end. This is especially true if someone dies in the year, because in the year of death, the IRS may penalize the estate of the decedent, if at the end of the year, enough RMD was not distributed. The heir to the estate is then held accountable for this because if a taxpayer dies and the RMD for the year was not distributed by December 31, the beneficiary who inherits the IRA or retirement account must take the deceased taxpayer's distribution by year end and add to that the beneficiary's income. This can really mess up the beneficiary's tax situation that year. **Be sure you see Azmoneyguy or your tax professional as soon as possible after you find out you are inheriting retirement money!**

While taxes are not required to be withheld from distributions, remember to submit estimated taxes, by the deadline to pay for this additional income on your tax return. Azmoneyguy or your tax professional knows these rules, so be sure you compute and distribute your RMD and any estimated income taxes before year end deadlines.

Moreover, you can choose to have your RMD given to any qualified charity. If you choose this route, you pay NO taxes on the amount given to the charity.

Caution, the penalty for not meeting the RMD is now 100% of the amount that should have been distributed, plus interest!
For some taxpayers, taking money out a retirement account is something you dread because it means that you have no choice,

financially, but to distribute funds from retirement accounts. This can happen when you find yourself in dire financial straits, like a pending foreclosure on your house! If you are under the age of 59 ½ you could be penalized by the Internal Revenue Service for taking premature distributions. Depending on the type of retirement account you have, the penalty can range from 10% - 25%.

But, not to worry. There is penalty relief, for those under 59 ½, if you withdraw or distribute money from retirement accounts for very specific reasons!

Here are some ways to take money out of a retirement account WITHOUT having to pay a penalty, if you are under 59 ½ years old by the end of the year:

- **Death** (monies paid to beneficiaries from retirement accounts)

- **Divorce** (money paid to an ex-spouse as part of a divorce or Qualified Domestic Relations Order)

- **Disability** (if you take money out because you are totally disabled)

- **Education expenses** (distributing money for education expenses for you or your dependents)

- **Medical expenses** (medical expenses paid above 7 ½% of your income)

- **Medical insurance if you are unemployed** (paying your Health insurance is allowed in the year you are unemployed for 2 months or longer)

- **You live in a Federal Declared Disaster area** (taking money out of retirement to replace items not covered by insurance)

- **Equal distributions over remaining life** (taking money out of a retirement account equally over the remaining years of your life). The IRS uses a table to determine the minimum amount to be withdrawn, based on your age at the time you start withdrawing funds.

- **Down payment on a house** (you can withdraw up to $10,000 to buy a home if you have not owned one in the last 2 years).

- **Birth or Adoption of a child** costs are allowed as an exception to the penalty, up to $10,000, per parent total.

- **Paying back taxes to IRS** because of a Levy filed.

- **Distributions to qualified Military** (reservists) called to active duty (Deployments)

- **Rollovers from one retirement plan to another** allows you up to 60 calendar days to deposit funds into the new retirement plan.

- **Separation from work at 55 or later** allows you to retire early, take distributions from retirement plans and not be penalized.

Here are six things from the IRS, that you should also know about EARLY withdrawals from retirement accounts:

1. An early withdrawal normally means taking money from your plan before you reach age 59½.

2. If you made a withdrawal from a plan last year, you must report the amount to the IRS. You may have to pay income tax as well as an additional penalty tax on the amount of withdrawal.

3. The additional tax does not apply to nontaxable withdrawals. Nontaxable withdrawals include withdrawals of your cost to participate in the plan. Your cost includes contributions that you paid tax on before you put them into the plan. Or funds contributed to the plan that did not receive a tax deduction for doing it.

4. A rollover is a type of nontaxable withdrawal. Generally, a rollover is a distribution to you of cash or other assets from one retirement plan that you contribute to another retirement plan. You usually have 60 calendar days to complete a rollover to make it tax- free.

5. There are many exceptions to the 10% additional penalty tax. Some of the exceptions for retirement plans are different for each type of plan. See the bullet points mentioned earlier, Azmoneyguy or your tax professional to see if any exceptions apply to your situation.

6. If you make an early withdrawal, you may need to file **Form 5329**, Additional Taxes on Qualified Plans (Including IRAs) and Other Tax-Favored Accounts, with your federal tax return.

7. Finally, remember that you may be penalized up to 100% of the required minimum distribution if you do NOT take out enough from your retirement account once you reach age 72.

52 WAYS TO
OUTSMART THE IRS:

Made in the USA
Middletown, DE
05 October 2022